53 SP 45
November 2023
Brooklyn, NY

Angela's Mixtape + The History of Light
© Eisa Davis 2023
53rdstatepress.org

ISBN Number: 978-1732545298
Library of Congress Number: 2023943443

Book design: Kate Kremer
Cover design: w/d

Printed on recycled paper in the United States of America.

Angela's Mixtape + The History of Light is made possible by the New York State Council on the Arts with the support of the Office of the Governor and the New York State Legislature.

ANGELA'S MIXTAPE

EISA DAVIS

THE HISTORY OF LIGHT

53rd State Press
Brooklyn, NY

"...an engaging new free-form autobiographical show...an affectionate tribute to her aunt as well as a memoir of her own unusual upbringing, *Angela's Mixtape* is a rhythmic collage of scenes, songs and reminiscences. This appropriately turbulent and quite funny show about the forces that influence the forging of identity...[is] rich in humor and crazy paradox...the strange juxtaposition of the prosaic trials of adolescence and the urgent radicalism of the family politics is what gives the show its own distinctive identity."

—*The New York Times*

"...transports audiences back several decades to a moment in history with eerie echoes forward into the present. Themes of the fight against racism, economic inequality, and oppression are as alive now as they were then. The central theme, the painful and confusing quest for identity, is timeless...*Angela's Mixtape* is a wild ride in a time machine, a tough story told with love, humor and wisdom."

—*MV Times*

"It's lucky for us that Eisa Davis grew up to be an actor and a playwright (and a singer and a dancer) rather than a radical like her aunt Angela; otherwise we wouldn't have been so thoroughly entertained by her play, a wacky depiction of growing up an innocent around sixties revolutionaries...A revealing portrait of a young artist struggling to find herself...The cast of five women, including the multitalented playwright, is fully committed to what might be the Obama generation's *For Colored Girls Who Have Considered Suicide When the Rainbow Is Enuf.*"

—*The New Yorker*, Best of
Off-Broadway Theatre 2009

ANGELA'S MIXTAPE

EISA DAVIS

THE HISTORY OF LIGHT

"There is a famed quote by Arundhati Roy, 'another world is possible, she is on her way. On a quiet day, I can hear her breathing.' Might other worlds, other configurations exist alongside us already? Might the choices reported occlude other choices made? In the case of the United States of America, there remain hidden histories, realities, and future dreams that signal from outside the fray, that call to us to remember other degrees of perception, and that prod us out of the bottleneck. Eisa Davis has been here all along. *Angela's Mixtape* is a so-fresh tale of intersecting multiple truths, belonging to another world, wherein love in action, through the most challenging human circumstances, reframes change to say, 'she's good.'"

—Daniel Alexander Jones

"More than a half century after the anchoring events in *Angela's Mixtape*, I deeply appreciate the care with which Eisa constructed the multiple levels of meaning in this play. As an inspiration for one of the characters, I find that her skillful writing opens up the possibility to find humor, but also deep meaning, in struggle, and her creative use of the mixtape form offers new ways to examine the relationship between history, family, art and politics. But most of all, I remain immensely proud of my brilliant and talented niece, whose art continues to usher in new possibilities for cultural work to transform our world."

—Angela Y. Davis

To my family

My grandmother Sallye B. Davis holding me at three months, speaking at a rally for Angela's freedom. Photo by John Stayman.

CONTENTS

FOREWORD | LIESL TOMMY

I've been directing plays, film, and television for several decades now, and I consider the privilege of directing the great works of Eisa Davis to be career highlights.

Angela's Mixtape came first, then *The History of Light*. Both plays searingly and delicately told—at the time relatively unexplored on the stage—stories about the cost of being in a revolutionary family.

Eisa and I became artistic soul sisters as we shared parallel childhoods—hers in America, mine in Apartheid-era South Africa. We are both daughters of a revolution, both raised by profoundly committed Marxist activist parents. We shared so much.

But it was Eisa who found the words to describe what I always thought was the indescribable. She found a way to make the pride, chaos, fear, silence, rage, joy, and confusion throb on the page. She did it with poetic effortlessness. Eisa's genius as a writer flowered in front of my eyes with these plays.

Eisa inhabits power and fragility as a person. She fearlessly lets her characters share in those traits so subtly that, as a director, I sometimes wept in rehearsal for no reason other than I was watching the deepest truth and nuance unfold just from people saying those Eisa Davis words.

In our time it is brave for a Black woman to claim delicacy, to claim softness, but in both of these plays Eisa not only claimed these emotions but also explored them! Inhabited them! The intellectual rigor and emotional excavation she embedded inside the central conflicts were also such a thrill to unpack. The actors and I felt we were in the presence of a secret history. But of course it was American History, our shared history. We felt privileged to breathe walking and talking life into those pulsing pages.

And then there was the music. It really ain't right that such a writer as Eisa should also be anointed with that voice, those virtuosic piano playing skills, and the ability to compose music too?? But she was given the gift of music and she covered us in that pulse, that throb and that blessing all through these plays. I felt the audience get transported to that other dimension every night with the complex crafting of these plays with music.

No one else does what she does; no one else has the endless capacity to love and express love like she does. Because inside of these plays she expresses the essential truths of every real-ass revolutionary: the relentless, unshakeable love for all humanity, the wrenching compulsion to help everyone get free. And she put it in words.

I am so happy that you lucky readers will get to experience that pulse, that throb, that delicate truth poetry love bomb that is an Eisa Davis work. So take a breath and open your senses to the joys found in *Angela's Mixtape* and *The History of Light*.

—Liesl Tommy

ANGELA'S
MIXTAPE

Angela sitting with my cousin Cecilie Davis Carter on the porch in Birmingham

VOICE MESSAGE | CECILIE DAVIS CARTER

From a voice message (or several) from my cuz Cecilie Davis Carter.

○

I couldn't remember initially when we did the first reading of *Angela's Mixtape*, so I had to go online, but I do remember that it was at the Hip Hop Theater Festival. And I remember it was Danny Hoch and Kamilah Forbes who started it. I remember that before we did our reading we went to a bunch of shows. And it was so great. I'm trying to remember. I mean like a bunch of 'em. A bunch of 'em. And my mom was in town, and your mom was in town, but before they came, it was just you and me. And we had a lot of practice readings with the cast. I remember just being so excited because I had never been around theatre that had a hip hop rhythmic feel to it. I had never seen theatre like that before. And it was amazing. It was theatre with singing, rapping. It was poetry with that hip hop rhythm to it. And to be able to be part of that...

And I remember that t shirt which I still have with a Brooklyn skyline or NYC skyline on the front of the t shirt. And it said the NYC Hip Hop Theater Festival. And I felt so—it felt just really great to be a part of it. And I remember the practices. I remember... One of the practices—I remember it was in a room—it felt like gym bleachers. And it was the first time I met the other cast members. And I remember feeling a little bit nervous, a little insecure. Then I had to check myself. Like calm down. The character you are playing is Cess with two S's, you can't mess it up.[*]

---

[*]   I had named the character for Cecilie "CESS" with two S's not

After I talked myself off the ledge, I remember it being so much fun. Just a lot. A lot of fun. I remember it being really thick. The script. Like there were a lot of pages. And that scared me. But then again I talked myself off another ledge. We were just reading it with the stands in front of us and the scripts in front of us and it was going to be okay.

I don't remember how many rehearsals we had, but it was a bunch. And I do believe I had the script prior to us rehearsing together. But I do remember that feeling I had, and it was a feeling of just being alive. Like I felt energized just because I was in New York, performing. And up until that point I had not done any kind of performing outside of LA or Cleveland. So to be in New York, and preparing to be on a stage, and to perform a piece about our family in front of audiences during a hip hop theater festival was something again that I had never even—I couldn't even conceptualize because it was so new. Was beyond amazing. I literally had an electric feeling in my bones.

And I remember staying at your apartment which was great, and this was the apartment where—I'm trying to remember, there's been a few...this one had the long hallway that led back to your bedroom and your work area. And then the kitchen was in front of the work area I believe, and then there was the bathroom right across from the door. And you were like "Look. Soon as you come in this door, take your shoes off. We're walking throughout New York City. I mean you should just do it anywhere, but specifically in New York City. Where all throughout the city there is grossness." It was that apart-

---

knowing that Cecilie liked her name to be shortened to CES with only one S. I did not know about this preference for years. I've corrected the spelling to CES for this publication so her name is immortalized in the way that she wants!

ment I believe. And I remember there being books everywhere. And I remember your closet was small? But you made it work. Like you had your t shirts folded up in the tiniest Marie Kondo pre-Marie Kondo way so that everything could fit. I was truly amazed to be honest. Like I was lightweight impressed. Anyhoo. I remember being at your apartment and us just reading through these lines, just reading 'em reading 'em reading 'em reading 'em. And you know what, looking back on it, it was so cool of you, because it's like, I'm in your space, you're in a point in your career where you're kinda just getting started in this way. I mean you clearly had written plays, multiple plays, but this was kinda the beginning of your journey with this level of playwriting, like post-grad school, and I just, that was just so cool to share your space with me, and to be able to you know, nurture someone who was new, not only to New York City, but new to the whole entertainment / TV / film / theatre / literary, that whole, just new to it all. So thank you.

I remember I remember practicing. We had at least, I wanna say, at least three to five rehearsals before performing the show, and I remember watching all the other shows and going damn this is great. This is great. And it was a little intimidating. But like I said before, I was playing myself so, you know, I had to talk myself off the ledge. But not only that, it's like this is the introduction, this is the invitation into our world, our family, and to an audience and clearly nothing like this has ever been done before? I mean yes there had been pieces on Angela, but it's never been done by a family member, and that's giving people, audience members, a bird's eye view into what life is like being A, a family member of Angela Davis, B, a different perspective on Angela's life, and C, us just being vulnerable. So it was pretty heavy to be a part of something like that. And I remember in my head just telling myself, you're gonna be great, it's gonna be fine. And it was! It was so cool. It really was.

And I remember the day of our performance, you sent me there alone on the subway, and you were like you're gonna be fine. Like here's your card, your MTA card—is it MTA? MTA. Anyway. It was the subway card? And you told me exactly where to go. And you were like it's gonna be fine. And it was. I felt so good, I felt so grown up, I felt so grown up to be able to take the train from Fort Greene, yeah you were in Fort Greene, Clinton Hill, wherever you were in Brooklyn, I think you've always been in Fort Greene, yes? From Fort Greene into Manhattan. I felt like a grownup, like a big girl in the city, doing my thing. I remember being a little nervous taking the train alone, and you know I was nervous I was gonna get lost, and none of that happened. It was fine, I didn't get lost, I got on the right train, I made the right turns, and I got there. I made my way to the theatre just fine. Everything was cool.

And the jackets. The *Angela's Mixtape* jackets. I believe you gave us the jackets before the very first performance. Right? And again it just felt unreal. It felt surreal and it felt unreal. And you know Eis, we did a bunch of readings. We did readings in New York. And we did readings in Oakland right? I feel like we did both New York and Oakland.* And so a lot of the memories are merging together. But I remember it being so great just being on the stage and being in front of an audience. And singing and dancing. And people laughing. And we had a lotta laughs. A lotta laughs. Gollee.

When it was finally produced in New York years later, I remember walking into the venue where the show was. And the first person I saw was Ellen Burstyn. And I was like "Oh my god, that's Ellen Burstyn." And I was like "Hi Ellen Burs-

---

* I gave out customized *Angela's Mixtape* sweatshirts from Neighborhoodies when we performed at La Peña in Berkeley.

tyn." I didn't say her whole name, but it just was like wow this is amazing! And I am such a fan of hers. But I remember you telling me that she was one of your instructors, right? Wasn't she one of your teachers in grad school?[*] I remember you giving me the official introduction. And seeing my friend Paloma there, [the choreographer] Paloma McGregor. We were in a show together in Cleveland. And she was like oh my gosh, of course this is your family. I was like, yes, yes! I'm also remembering that Alicia Keys came.[**]

I remember being really happy to be there. And being able to be there with Angela and your mom...this was exciting. 'Cause it's the real people, the real characters. And it was so amazing, seeing the show. However, I wanted to be a part of it. I wanted to be in it.[***] But you know, as I got older I realized that things, there is a reason for everything. But a selfish moment watching the show was, "Hm! Why can't I play me?" But my life had changed since the beginning of us workshopping the show, you know? My life had changed. I had met Renard and we had gotten serious. And there were no kids, but you know, I lived in LA. It was just different. And I get that. And at that very moment I wanted to still be a part of it because it was such a meaningful and amazing show. But I eventually got it. I was able to look past that while watching the show, I really was, and I actually was able to enjoy the show in a different way, because any other time that I had quote unquote seen the show, was by being on stage. I'd never been able to watch it. And it was different. It was different. And I was able to enjoy

---

[*]   Yes. A mentor.

[**]   As a fan of everything Angela Davis, she came to a performance later in the run.

[***]   Cecilie made the difficult decision not to participate in the New York production.

it without having to make sure that I wasn't overacting, make sure I wasn't enunciating incorrectly, you know, the whole acting thing. I was able to just relax and watch a show. And there's levels to this thing. Because not only did I enjoy it, I was watching our characters, our real life characters on stage.

This is the only time in my life that I've been able—that I've had the opportunity to be a part, that my character, who I am, has been a part of any storyline that I can watch, let alone anybody can watch. You know? It's never happened. So thank you because it was just like, wow! And the gravity of it just is really heavy. Because you wrote a show. And the characters were yourself, because you were you. I mean of course it's gonna be you. Aunt Angela, of course, because it's *Angela's Mixtape*. Your mom, of course. 'Cause it's your mom. Your aunt Angela's sister. Your grandma. Of course. It's your grandma. Such a major part of your life. But then your cousin Ces? Whoa. Thank you. Like it's a big whoa. It's like wow. I am and have been a big part of your life and I appreciate that.

And I think it wasn't until—I mean I've known that, just like you're a big part of my life, however it didn't really hit me, it didn't really hit me hit me until I was able to watch the show on the outside. Looking in. It made a really big difference because it was like whoa. 'Cause like when you're in it—I had this one acting teacher, he used to say, actors are all inside the fishbowl with water in their eyes. And they can't see things. Whereas outside of the fishbowl you can see better because you're on the outside looking in, and you don't have water in your eyes. Well that's how I felt. As an audience member, as an observer, as the real character, it was so moving, so incredibly moving to be able to watch the play and at the same time realize how much of an impact we've had on each other, but in this case, me on you, to be able to write me in as a character in this show. I mean it was really like whoa. And I felt it. I felt it that day, whether I told you or not, and if I didn't, I'm sorry. But I felt it. I felt it like wow.

And I really enjoyed Ayesha's performance. Like she really did Ces with two s's, she did her well. (*Laughter.*) She did Ces really well. And I appreciated it. And I remember afterwards the flowers and the pictures of all of us and it's still on the internet today. "Eisa Davis' real life family comes to the show." That is so dope. And it's not even because people know I'm a part of the show, my name is out there, not like that, who cares about that. But again. It goes back to a deeper level of it all. You know these are the people who have had serious impact on Eisa. And obviously there are others, but as far as like this material and this part of your life? It was moving, man. It was so moving. And it was great to see.

And we all loved it. Like afterwards we all were like, oh my gosh how amazing. No! We're not mad at you, Eisa, this is awesome! I love that this is happening for the show now. I mean you deserve it. We all do. But yeah. People can say your private life is out there. But it's not private life that you don't want anyone to know. If anyone is being put on display, more than anyone it's you. 'Cause it's your stories. Um and I love the stories that you have told. I really do. I love all the stories, I love seeing the characters, I love the songs, I love the quickness of the show, I love the pace. Not many people had done these types of hip hop lyric driven type of shows. And it was so cool. It's almost like you're the historian of the family. Which is awesome. It really is. Okay. Let me know if this will suffice. Otherwise, I will give you more. Love you. Bye.

—Cecilie Davis Carter

IT'S ANGELA'S MIXTAPE Y'ALL | EISA DAVIS

What of your family legacy do you take with you and what do you leave behind?

o

2001, 2002, 2003 brought a huge rush of expression after a major relationship ended and a significant friendship was repaired. After our world battened down its hatches after the violence of and in response to September 11. After becoming a resident playwright at New Dramatists. After taking a road trip with my father. I was transforming on a cellular level. I was writing poems, singing and playing my music in concert more, internal changes leaving me almost giddy with a new sense of openness and possibility in life. I wrote *Bulrusher* during this time. And in a solo performance workshop steered by the genius Michael John Garcés, a friend and brilliant writer who had directed readings of my work, I began discovering the material that would jumpstart *Angela's Mixtape*. I talked to Adrienne Kennedy, my first playwriting teacher during my undergrad years at Harvard, and in whose stage memoir *June and Jean in Concert* I'd gotten my Actors' Equity card. At age 92, who with her piercing, original work has restructured the landscape of world theatre, Adrienne also remains a constant correspondent and a cherished mentor who compulsively urges me to champion my own writing. I had written a one-act in Adrienne's class called *Dynamite Hill*, revealing how as children my cousins and I were unaware of the extent of the violence that had taken place on the Birmingham, Alabama soil around our grandparents' home, the ground on which we played so jubilantly. It was without a doubt a survivor's guilt play, and Adrienne had called it a gold mine. So when I talked to her about wanting to write more

Opposite: Me, Angela, my mother Fania facing us at the San Jose Courthouse, 1972.

about my family and about my aunt Angela, she encouraged me to do it—reminding me I'd already written a number of other plays and that it was okay to write autobiographically now. She had revolutionized the form of the memoir by reimagining it as an annotated scrapbook, and continued to give her family more and more mythic freight in each play. I would write about my family—in a memoir form shot through with hip hop—with the same reverence.

The Hip Hop Theater Festival was a new, necessary, and urgent vector for innovative performance founded by pioneers Danny Hoch, Kamilah Forbes, and Clyde Valentin. I had written an article for *The Source* in 2000 about this fresh, hybrid genre that thrilled me and welcomed me into its nexus, thus playing a small role in bringing together a community that included artists like Universes, Sarah Jones, Will Power, Toni Blackman, Jonzi D, Psalmayene 24, Rennie Harris, Lisa Jessie Peterson, Kristoffer Diaz, Nilaja Sun, Ben Snyder, and Chadwick Boseman, who were all part of the festival's first blazing years. Michael John Garcés and I had staged a reading of my play *Umkovu* in 2001 at the festival, DJed by the legendary Bobbito, and in 2003, Clyde Valentin asked me if I had a new piece for their reading series. I said sure, even though I had nothing on tap. He asked for a blurb. I told him, "I think I'm going to write about growing up with my aunt Angela." Got a blurb? "Even red-diaper babies have to go to prom."

So I sat at my tiny wooden kitchen table with that blurb and wrote a play. I wanted to make something that would feel like a hip hop mixtape, but also like the living room shows I used to put on as a child with help from my sister Kafí and cousin Cecilie and neighbors and other cousins. A piece that could bring to life all the hilarious and her-storic experiences of our family that were bursting out of me. I wrote as fast as I could. I ended up with a stack of pages way longer than the ninety-minute version in this book. Cecilie came out to New York to act in that first reading in June 2003, and my mother and my aunt Sylvia, Cecilie's mother, came to support us from the audience. One night after rehearsal, Cecilie and I went to see the LAByrinth Theater Company's production of Stephen Adly Guirgis' *Our Lady of 121st Street*, directed by Philip Seymour Hoffman. That legendary original cast including Ron Cephas Jones, David Zayas, Liza Colon-Zayas, Portia, Russell G. Jones, Elizabeth Canavan, Scott Hudson, Mark Hammer, Melissa Feldman, John Ortiz, Felix Solis, and Richard Petrocelli taught the world how immediate and potent theater could be. The show had a rawness and honesty and excellence that felt like the epitome of New York, just what I had come to the city to be a part of. I wanted to ascend to their level of artistry.

Michole Briana White and Angela Bullock played Angela and my mother, respectively, for that first reading at New York Theater Workshop. What a rush. And Lynn Nottage came and gave a perfect note about not switching the POV away from myself. I invited my mother and my aunt Sylvia on stage afterwards and my mother had notes too! She let the audience know right then and there what she disagreed with in my depiction of her. And in the next draft, I folded her version of the events into the text, embracing the contradiction in our memories, making the conflict our dialogue.

I was clamoring to get the play produced right away. People who saw readings said wow, seems like you really needed to say this! But theatres didn't feel the same. We did five years of readings at Second Stage, The Culture Project, The Kitchen, New Dramatists, The University of Utah (where they could not find any Black actresses, so the cast was made up of Black women who had never sung or performed before. Instead, they came from jobs in administration or other professions around the campus. After a lot of courageous rehearsals, they were fantastic!). We did a reading in Berkeley at La Peña around the corner from where I grew up. And then in 2006 we did a workshop at New York Theater Workshop's Dartmouth retreat. The artistic leadership at NYTW, Jim Nicola and Linda Chapman, were interested in a piece about Angela Davis, and suggested Liesl Tommy to me as a director. I was a little hesitant to work with someone whose work I hadn't seen. Then we started talking, and immediately I found a new sister in her. With our similar upbringings, we connected instantly on a profound level. In our wide-ranging late night talks about growing up in our warrior households and finding refuge in theatre, the play began to speak uncannily for both of us as movement babies. When two theatres finally offered to produce a rolling world premiere, she was down for it all. So let me stop this preamble and list the names of the people and places who did the productions then you can finally read this play!

—Eisa Davis

Angela and me

PRODUCTION HISTORY

Angela's Mixtape was produced at Synchronicity Performance Group at 7 Stages in Atlanta from February 15 – March 16, 2008, by artistic director Rachel May. It was directed by Liesl Tommy.

Cast

GRANDMA/VARIOUS | Greta Glenn
CES/VARIOUS | Jeanette Illidge
MOMMY | Naomi Lavette
EISA | Ayesha Jordan
ANGELA | Minka Wiltz

Designers + Crew

Stage Manager | Laura Coates
Props Designer | Kate Bidwell
Lighting Designer | Jessica Coale
Costume Designer | Nyrobi Moss
Set Designer | Rochelle Barker
Sound Designer | Spencer Stephens
Production Manager | Jon Summers
Master Electrician | Marie Dunn
Technical Director | Eric VanArsdale
Piano Teacher | Caroline Masclet

Angela's Mixtape premiered in New York at the Ohio Theatre in a co-production by New Georges, Susan Bernfield, artistic director, and the Hip Hop Theater Festival, Kamilah Forbes, artistic director, and Clyde Valentin, executive director, April 9 – May 2, 2009. It was directed by Liesl Tommy.

Cast

MOMMY | Kim Brockington
GRANDMA/OTHERS | Denise Burse
EISA | Eisa Davis
CES/OTHERS | Ayesha Jordan
ANGELA | Linda Powell

Design + Production

Costumes | Jessica Jahn
Sound | Jane Shaw
Scenic Design | Clint Ramos
Lights | Sarah Sidman
Production Photos + Press | Jim Baldassare

Angela's Mixtape was subsequently produced at the Vineyard Playhouse on Martha's Vineyard July 21 – August 11, 2018, directed by Adrienne D. Williams.

CHARACTERS

Five black women:

EISA
ANGELA
MOMMY
CES
GRANDMA

GRANDMA and CES play all of the other characters.

CHORUS = multiple voices, sometimes all, sometimes some.

NOTES

The play is a mixtape, jumping from one song/scene to the next, proceeding primarily by rhythm or melody. The pace rarely, if ever, drops below 100 beats per minute. The text is not only spoken, but also danced and sung. Past, present, and future all happen at once. The mixtape is less story, more state of mind; time and place shift as fluidly and as quickly as thoughts.

Opposite: Fania, Angela, me, and Cecilie (top). The Mixtape ladies: Linda Powell, Ayesha Jordan, Liesl Tommy, me, Denise Burse, Kim Brockington (below).

MOMMY, ANGELA, GRANDMA *and* CES
enter wilding out, hyping the crowd.

CES

(*running around the stage*) Angela's Mixtape, y'all! What up!

> EISA *enters and inserts a cassette into*
> *the boombox. She grabs a hairbrush*
> *to use as a mic.*

EISA

On this mixtape, style will dictate,
we bounce back and forth in time.
Mom, Grandma, Auntie and Cuz
are here to help me with my lines.
I care enough to send the very best,
so I'll find tunes to play the part
Of my memories, linked up reveries,
sync 'em up press record and start.

> *A red light goes on to indicate we are*
> *recording. "122 BPM" plays.*

EISA

I'm a say it again but different. Watch me now!
On this mixtape, style will dictate,
we bounce back and forth in time.
Angela fights for who's behind bars,
but she's free, the bars are mine.
I am her namesake, but wear a different face,
I watch and learn all I can.
Mom makes the rules, Ces plays the fool,
but I don't know who I am.

MOMMY + GRANDMA
(*Black Power salute*) Free Angela!

EISA
With the shame of fame, on the blame terrain,
how do I live up to my name?

MOMMY + GRANDMA + CES
Free Angela!

EISA
How do I live up to my name?

MOMMY + GRANDMA + CES
Free Angela!

EISA
How do I live up to my name?

MOMMY + GRANDMA + CES
Free Angela!

> EISA *cuts "122 BPM" out.*

CES

Let's kick this off with an old school joint.

> *All the actors sing the bassline and snap*
> *to George Benson's "On Broadway".*
> *They continue under* EISA's *lines.*

EISA

The first time I ever set foot in New York City, I got off the
6 train at Bleecker Street and they were shooting a movie!
Ghostbusters 2. I was staying in Greenwich Village on Sul-
livan Street with my college friend and his parents and they
seemed just like New York to me.

> EISA *pulls out* ANGELA's *autobiography,*
> *looks around.*

Angela used to go to school near here, her book says. On this trip, I read her autobiography cover to cover for the first time. I am nineteen. Who is this woman everyone loves?

> *They stop the bassline to "On Broadway".* EISA *reads from Angela's book.*

On October 13th, 1970, Angela was arrested and imprisoned at the Women's House of Detention on Greenwich and Sixth Avenues.

ANGELA
"Walking to the subway station after school, I used to look up at this building every day, trying not to listen to the terrible noises spilling from the windows. They were coming from the women locked behind bars, screaming incomprehensible words."

EISA
(*looking up at the tower*) The clock tower's still here but no prison. Demolished in '73, replaced with a library and a garden.

ANGELA
"I never knew what to do when I saw the outlines of women's heads through the almost opaque windows of the jail. I could never understand what they were saying— whether they simply wanted to talk to anyone who was 'free.' Would I scream out at the people passing in the streets, only to have them pretend not to hear me as I once pretended not to hear those women?"

EISA
(*singing softly*)
Oh we don't care if we go to jail
It is for freedom that we gladly go.
Oh we don't care if we go to jail
It is for freedom that we gladly go.
(*repeat as needed*)

CHORUS	EISA
Oh we don't care if we go to jail	*Oh we don't care if we go to jail*
It is for freedom that we gladly go	*It is for freedom that we gladly go*
Oh we don't care if we go to jail	*A heavy load,*
It is for freedom that we gladly go	*a heavy load*
	And it will take some real strength

> *Sound of prison doors slamming as* ANGELA *is arrested. We see her in handcuffs in the blue light of the jail.*

EISA
I never knew this. No knowledge, no gratitude.

> *Rewind/scratching sounds as* EISA *releases the autobiography to* MOMMY. *A song from 1990 plays—maybe "Back to Life" by Soul II Soul.*

ID

PORTER (GRANDMA)
Name?

EISA
Eisa Davis, on the 9 o'clock flight to New York.

PORTER
Photo ID. (*She hands it over.*) Angela Davis, huh.

EISA
(*to* AUDIENCE) This happens every day. College ID, charge cards...

PORTER
What?

EISA
Angela, yeah.

PORTER
You just said Eisa Davis.

EISA
People call me Eisa.

CES
(*sings*) *Ain't nobody gonna breaka my stride*

EISA
Remember that song?

PORTER
But your ID says Angela.

EISA
My first name is Angela.

PORTER
But people call you Eisa.

EISA
Yeah, that's my name. Angela Eisa Davis.

CES
(*sings*) *Nobody's gonna hold me down*

PORTER
You don't like Angela?

EISA
Eisa's my middle name.

PORTER
Exactly. Angela Davis. That's—heavy.

EISA
I know.

PORTER
You're not her are you? 'Cause you kind of look like her.

EISA
Yeah my fist kinda balls up into the same shape.

> EISA *does the Black Power salute.*

PORTER
Your hair is a little small for that though.

EISA
She's my aunt. Are my bags going to make it?

PORTER
No shit.

CES
(*sings*) *Oh no*

EISA
No?

PORTER
She's your aunt? Wow. How is she?

EISA
Good.

PORTER

I had a crush on her when I was a kid. That FBI Ten Most
Wanted poster, mm. And you know they showed that photo
on TV all the time. Wow. What's she doing now?

EISA + CES

(*sings*) *I've got to keep on movin—*

EISA

What she's always done. Teach.

PORTER

In LA, right?

EISA

No, Santa Cruz. I don't want to miss my flight.

> *An oval light on* EISA, *as if she is look-
> ing out a plane window. Plane engine
> purrs.*

EISA

Do *you* know who she is?
The Angela I know used to blowdry my hair and french braid
it. She pegged my pants on her sewing machine so I would be
in style. And she used to make me mixtapes with Keith Jarrett
and Billie Holiday. (*scratching her line*) This mixtape th-th-
this mixtape th-th this mixtape is for her.

GRANDMA + CES

You are born Angela Eisa Davis, the child of two sisters, in
Berkeley, California.

> *Lights change.* EISA *plays the mbira, a
> Zimbabwean thumb piano.*

BERKELEY: THE '70s

> MOMMY *is laughing with a friend on a phone and talking with* EISA *on the side.*

MOMMY
(*to* EISA) Do you want some weed? Just kidding.

> EISA *stops playing the mbira.*

EISA
What's a nymphomaniac?

MOMMY
A person who loves sex. A person who loves to have sex all the time!

EISA
Do you love sex?

MOMMY
I enjoy it.

EISA
(*to* AUDIENCE) My mother loves sex!

MOMMY
I'm NOT a nymphomaniac. Where did you hear that word?

EISA
She keeps our doors open. We often walk naked through the house.

MOMMY
(*to friend on phone*) One time this guy walked in and tried to rape me and I yelled at him! I yelled and ran him down the street!

EISA

Our new next door neighbors are holistic health specialists.

EISA plays the mbira again.

NEIGHBOR (GRANDMA)

I paint mandalas, I teach yoga, I make meals with the Moose-
wood cookbook. I have two daughters named Gaia and
Rainbow. I grow marijuana in the closet upstairs but Rainbow
thinks they're tomato plants.

EISA

Their dog is named Ganesha but Rainbow calls him Furry.

NEIGHBOR

I'm Polish and have hair down to my waist. I use a sea sponge
as a tampon. I love *Mork and Mindy* and watch it every
Tuesday.

EISA

At the Christmas crafts fair in Berkeley she sells baskets she's
made out of pine needles and sea kelp.

NEIGHBOR

I sunbathe naked in the backyard, and Fania and Eisa can see
me from their dining room table. We drive our VW bus down
to Baja every summer. I had Gaia naturally in a water birth,
and we all take hot tubs naked with the dog. I nursed Rainbow until she was 6.

EISA stops playing the mbira.

EISA

Rainbow's going to be on my radio show. Her and my cousin
Cecilie. She's visiting. (EISA *speaks into mic;* CES *joins her on
the last words of each sentence.*) And here's your host Eisa!
Welcome to our show. And now for a commercial break!

(sings) *"Your Tupperware lady has the freshest ideas—for locking in (snaps twice) freshness."*

The sound of a blender.

MOMMY
Don't sing commercials in the house—don't sing them at all.

EISA
Mom, we're recording, turn off the blender!

MOMMY
I'm making smoothies, don't you want one?

EISA
Can we have french toast with apple butter for dinner tonight?

MOMMY
Okay, after your miso. I've just chopped all the vegetables up. When you're done recording come out and I'll give you a quiz on what part of your body each vegetable is good for!

EISA
My mom makes being poor so much fun! Every morning after my oatmeal but before school, we sneak into Lake Anza to swim.

The lake is brown

CHORUS
The lake is brown

EISA
We're going down

CHORUS
We're going down

EISA

To swim in the morning with no delay
Reach the raft in the middle then turn away
Flip the tricks underwater in sand we play
Mommy got us in the water to start the day
On weekends we go to demonstrations.

MOMMY
Eisa, wake up. It's time to go to the demonstration.

> CES *and* GRANDMA *pass out flyers—it*
> *is one of* ANGELA's *essays.*

EISA
(*the Black Panther chant*) Revolution has come!

CHORUS + EISA
Off the pig!

EISA
Time to pick up the gun!

CHORUS + EISA
Off the pig!

EISA
Mom, why is it called a demonstration? What are we demonstrating?

MOMMY
Our unity! We are showing people there is a mass movement and that we want social and economic justice for oppressed peoples all over the globe!

EISA
Who are oppressed people?

MOMMY

We are all oppressed as long as there is injustice.

EISA

We're oppressed? I thought we were the intelligentsia.

MOMMY

I am a lawyer, Eisa. But my work would mean nothing if I did not use the law to combat the racism and sexism and classism that this country was built on, if I did not use my life to fight for the cause. Every choice, every action, every waking moment is for liberation. Now eat your scrambled tofu and let's go. You're singing today.

EISA

(*tentative at first*) *We who believe in freedom cannot rest.*

CHORUS

We who believe in freedom cannot rest until it comes.

EISA

Until the killing of a black man, black mother's son
Is as important as the killing of a white man,
white mother's son.

CHORUS

We who believe in freedom cannot rest.
We who believe in freedom cannot rest.

ANGELA

"Compulsively almost, for hours at a time, I answer letter after letter from other prisoners. My very existence, it seems, is dependent on my ability to reach out to them. I have decided that if I am ever free, I will use my life to uphold the cause of my sisters and brothers behind walls."

BIRMINGHAM

Dear comrade, I was born in

Birming Birming Birming Birmingham
Burning Burning Burning Burningham
Bombing Bombing Bombing Bombingham

Some of us have never felt safe.
When they built city housing projects for our people,
whites got heat and toilets; Negroes got four walls.
I fought for fair treatment.
We got the toilets but not the heat.

I was born toward the end of the war
lived in the brick and love was thick till I blew out all four
candles, Mother could handle some birthday cake
flavor always tastes sweeter when you raise the stakes
ante up it's a gamble my father took
moved us out the projects to a whole new look
step right in to our house on the hill
hate is the local specialty and we're eating our fill
white paint, white teeth, white eyes, white fun
to bomb out the houses make the nigras run
we were the first speck of color here since slavery days
and we sure ain't the last
so Sundays blaze

Woke up this morning with my mind
Stayed on freedom

EISA *is on the floor, drawing.*

MOMMY
(*gently*) All the princesses you draw don't have to be white, you know. They can be black, brown, red, or yellow too.

EISA
I read books on Mahalia Jackson
Cuauhtemoc
Phyllis Wheatley
but the person I admired most was Paul Robeson.
He did everything.
Law, football, sang, acted, was an activist, a Communist.
That impressed me.
If we don't go to demonstrations on Saturdays, we go to dance class!

> *"Do Like You" by Stevie Wonder plays.*

DANCE TEACHER (CES)
(*carrying a picket sign, leading a dance warmup*) 5, 6, 7, and I-so-LA-TIONS. Let's take it back and forth. And back and forth. Shoulders up and down, up and down, take it back and front, back and front, hips circle yes, and yes, and yes, and yes reverse it...

> EISA, MOMMY, GRANDMA, *and* DANCE TEACHER *dance in unison.*

EISA
At Everybody's Creative Arts Center in Oakland, there's a wall painted like a real jungle and a belly dancer tattooed all over her body! She told my mom she was raped once. (*to* MOMMY) What does rape mean?

MOMMY

It's when a man takes sexual advantage of a woman by force. White slave masters did this to our ancestors daily. Keep your shoulders down! And chassé!

EISA

There is a bald woman who dances with us who played the Tornado in *The Wiz*! The smell of sweat everywhere, taped feet. Leg warmers and pants that look like big garbage bags. Leotards of cotton and polyester.

> *"Do Like You" out.* EISA, CES, GRAND-MA *and* MOMMY *march to the same beat they were dancing to.*

CHORUS
Socialismo, ho!
Socialism, ho!
Capitalismo, no!
Capitalism, no!

EDUCATION

STUDENT (CES)
The Hare Krishnas are here!

CHORUS
(*singing*) *Hare Krishna, Hare Krishna, Krishna Krishna, Hare Hare.*

EISA
The Hare Krishnas always walk by at 1pm singing so loud we have to stop whatever we are doing.

CHORUS + EISA
Hare Rama, Hare Rama Rama Rama, Hare Hare.

On the last "Hare," a schoolbell rings.

TEACHER (GRANDMA)
(*trying to pronounce name*) Angela Aisha Davis?

EISA
Here. You can just call me Eisa.

TEACHER
Alright then, Angela. I am your *history* teacher you know.

EISA
Yes.

STUDENT (CES)
Did you feel the earthquake last night?

EISA
No, I must've slept through it.

TEACHER
So Angela.

EISA
Yes.

TEACHER
Angela, I don't waste any opportunity to teach history, especially when I'm staring it in the eye. Your aunt is an important woman.

EISA
(*to* AUDIENCE) I know, but I don't really know why.
(*to* ANGELA) Angela, what happened to you when I was born? Why were you in jail? Why are you famous?

ANGELA
(*a pause, then*) Read the book.

TEACHER
Angela Davis is important.

EISA
What I know is Angela's house is always filled with people,
with women who care for me. One woman, Angela's and my
dance teacher, says I should always keep five dollars with me
in case of an emergency. Another woman writes me letters
and leaves them at my feet as I nap on Angela's bed. Another
woman builds things with wood. Another manages a copy
center and writes poetry, and another helps Angela schedule
her speeches and work at the university. I love talking with
them because they don't treat me like a child at all. They treat
me like a confidante.

What are you doing, Mom?

MOMMY
I'm meditating.

EISA
How do you do that?

MOMMY
Just sit quietly with me and you'll see how it's done.

Silence.

EISA
I am looking at the bedspread, the Indian print bedspread.
There is a red light bulb overhead.

EISA *raps—slowly at first, then faster.*

FIVE! minutes of funk, this ain't no junk...
I don't know if all of you have HEARD
so it's up to ME to spread the word
about the man that we feel has GOT to be real

(*mumbles made up lyric*) on the wheels a steel
he goes by the name of Grandmaster Dee
so if it's alright with you it's alright with me
we gonna rock you people's minds with ease
get some help from the maestro if you please
boom boom boom boom boom bump

MOMMY
Did you like meditating?

EISA
(*to* AUDIENCE) I don't know what I was doing.

MOMMY laughs.

EISA
She laughed.

BACK TO THE FUTURE

We hear "Jump" by Aretha Franklin.

EISA
We just went to see *Back to the Future*. My mom and I have a
debate afterwards. Not only do I express my opinion, I argue
against *her*, a lawyer, and hold my own!

(*to* MOM) My question is, remember toward the end of the
movie when Michael J. Fox comes back to the future *early*?
Remember? He comes back right before he left, and sees *himself* in the time machine car? How come he multiplied? Why
were there *two* of him?

MOMMY
Because he was outside of himself when he went time traveling.

EISA

But you're always yourself no matter where you are.

MOMMY

But *when* you are changes things. He wasn't in the fourth dimension, normal time, like he was before—he went into another dimension altogether.

EISA

But how can you be in two places at once?

MOMMY

He wasn't in two *places* at once, he was in two *time zones* at once. Like when we call Grandma in Birmingham from here in California. It's different times here and there on the clock, but it's the same moment on the phone.

EISA

But me and Grandma are two different people! (*hitting herself in the head*) "McFly!"

MOMMY

That's correct, but technically, so was he. He went back in time to talk to his parents, but he was already there as a sperm in his father and an egg in his mother. He broke the rules of time and space. That's the entire premise of the movie.

EISA

But that doesn't make sense. That means he's still two people and that's not what the movie is called. It's called *Back to the Future*, not *I Am Two People*. If he could become two people, one in normal time and one outside of it, they should have told us in the title. (*to* AUDIENCE) This is fun.

MOMMY

Movies aren't real.

EISA
But they shouldn't let you know they aren't real. (*then, her slam dunk*) After he changed the past, his old self can no longer exist! When he comes back to the future, he can only be *one* new self!

MOMMY
He didn't change. His parents did.

EISA
He changed by changing them!

MOMMY
(*looks at her*) It's a metaphor, Eisa, you have to look at it that way instead of literally.

EISA
(*a victory in her mind*) I know it's a metaphor, but it's not complete.

EGYPT

ANGELA *types with a clave rhythm.*

EISA
(*rapping and beatboxing*) Egypt, sss aaah
Egypt, sss aaah
you know it
and my beat goes

CES
(*overlapping, ad lib*) Oh this is my song, I gotta mix it up with

EISA + CES
Boom ch. Boom boom ch. Boom boom ch boom. Uh—uh—

HEAD (CES)
You want to make a rhyme?

EISA
I wanna rhyme!

HEAD
You've got to be hard.
You've got to boast about your crew.
You've got to talk about beating people up with your flow.
You've got to cap on people.

EISA
I'm the Egyptian Lover with the hard rock beat
jamming so hard I'll make your grandma freak

GRANDMA *observes them.*

HEAD
(*makes face at* EISA's *rhyme*) If you can't rhyme, you've got to
break.

EISA
I wanna break!

HEAD
Pop, lock, footwork, back and headspins.
(*makes face at* EISA's *breaking*) If you can't break, you've got
to have a name, a tag you can write on the bus bench and on
your locker and your notebook.

GRANDMA *dances the freak.*

HEAD
Or you can be a DJ and throw the parties but you have to
have a crew with matching pink sweatshirts with iron on
letters for that. (*beatbox and typing ends*) Sheeee-it.

GRANDMA

I know I didn't hear that. (*turning to* EISA) Did your grandmother just hear a four-letter word?

EISA

I practice cursing on my walk home. My grandma always told me

EVERYONE BUT EISA

God is watching you EVERYWHERE.

EISA

so it's physically impossible for me to form bad words with my mouth. Still, I want to learn how to curse.

ANGELA	EISA
"My mother never allowed anyone to say the word 'nigger' in the house."	F—, sh—, fuh—

GRANDMA

(*a chilling whisper*) Children! It's quiet time!

ANGELA

"For that matter, no 'bad words'—'shit,' 'damn,' not even 'hell' could be uttered in her presence. If we wanted to describe an argument we had had with someone, we had to say, 'Bill called me that bad word that starts with an n.' Eventually, my mouth simply refused to pronounce those words for me, regardless of how hard I might want to say them."

EISA *does a backspin.*

EISA

I need linoleum. (*without flavor*)
A change, a change has come over me

HEAD

Wait a minute, wait a minute. When you sing gospel, you move your mouth around to make the sound come out gospel-style.

EISA

(*with mouth movement*)
He changed my life complete
and now I sit, I sit at his feet

CHORUS

(*with mouth movement*)
To do what must be done
I'll work and work until it comes

MOMMY

(*to a Party member*) Well, I put her in a clown class, and she played an African healer at her school's cultural day.

EISA

I was a witch doctor!

MOMMY

Witch doctors don't exist, that's a colonialist notion. You'd think in Berkeley you wouldn't have to hear "witch doctor" anymore. So listen, she's so excited by theatre and performing and I think she should do some dramatic monologues about Angela's life at a Communist Party function. And she likes to sing too. Eisa, tell the story about when our family moved into the white neighborhood in Birmingham.

> EISA *begins.* MOMMY *follows along in the autobiography.*

EISA

(*bad, dramatic child acting*) "It was evening in the spring of 1949. I was in the bathroom washing my white shoelaces for Sunday School the next morning when an explosion a hundred times louder than the loudest, most frightening thunderclap I had ever heard shook our house. Medicine bottles fell off the shelves, shattering all around me. The floor seemed to slip away from my feet as I raced into the kitchen and into my frightened mother's arms.

"Crowds of angry Black people came up the hill and stood on 'our' side, staring at the bombed-out ruins of our neighbors' house. Of their own fear they said nothing. Apparently it did not exist, for Black families continued to move in. The bombings were such a constant response that soon our neighborhood became known as Dynamite Hill."

> EISA *bows. Everyone applauds.*

MOMMY
That was great! Wasn't that great? Do you want a carob cluster?

EISA
(*singing the theme to* The Smurfs) *La la la la la la…*

> *Everyone goes over to* ANGELA's *house.*
> *She tells a story.*

ANGELA
Eisa was playing with this boy outside and she came in crying. "He hurt me, he hurt me," she kept saying. We searched for bruises or blood. "Where did he hurt you?" we asked.

GRANDMA + ANGELA
"He hurt my feelings," Eisa said.

> *Everyone laughs except* EISA.

ANGELA
(*to* EISA) Want to try some caviar?

EISA
What's that?

ANGELA
Fish eggs. I got them in Moscow.

EISA
These eggs are black, not yellow.

ANGELA
They're fish, not chickens. Try it.

> *She spreads some on a cracker.* EISA
> *tries it and gags.* ANGELA *laughs. She*
> *stuffs her pipe, drinks port, and speaks*
> *from her autobiography.*

HAIR

ANGELA
"If, in the course of an argument with one of my friends, I was
called 'nigger' or 'black,' it didn't bother me nearly so much
as when somebody said, 'Just because you're bright and got
good hair, you think you can act like you're white.' Sometimes
I used to secretly resent my parents for giving me light skin
instead of dark, and wavy instead of kinky hair. I pleaded
with my mother to let me get it straightened, like my friends.
But she continued to brush it with water and rub vaseline in
it to make it lie down so she could fix the two big wavy plaits
(*pronounced platz*) which always hung down my back."

EISA
Mommy, I have to get a perm.

MOMMY
You don't need one.

EISA
Swimming! (*to* AUDIENCE) She cornrows my hair and when I get out of the water, I have nasty looking beebees on my hairline. I had to hide those braids under a hoodie for two weeks.

MOMMY
I don't straighten mine.

EISA
You don't need to. This nappy hair must be my father's. Who is he?

ANGELA
"One summer when our Brownie troop was at Camp Blossom Hill, it started to rain as we were walking from the mess hall to our cabins, and the girls' hands immediately went for their heads. The water was no threat to my unstraightened hair, so I paid no attention to the rain. One of the girls switched out and said:"

SWITCH GIRL (CES)
"'Angela's got good hair. She can stroll in the rain from now until doomsday.'"

ANGELA
"I ran back to my cabin, threw myself on the bunk sobbing."

MOMMY
A perm isn't healthy. The chemicals they put on your scalp are very close to your brain.
Ohhhh, freedom.
Ohhhh, freedom.
(*indicating hair*) *Ohhhh, freedom over me...*

KKK

WOMAN (CES)
(*hysterical*) They burned a cross on our lawn.

MOMMY
(*calm*) On what date?

EISA
I do my homework everywhere but home. Evenings, we're always at Party meetings, or I'm with Mommy and a client. The Ku Klux Klan is still alive and well in Contra Costa, just over the county line from Berkeley.

MOMMY
Approximately how many threatening phone calls have you received in the last month?

EISA
For school, I'm reading *The Autobiography of Miss Jane Pittman* and *Gone With The Wind*.

EISA *falls asleep.*

WOMAN
(*calmer*) They drove a truck through the plate glass window in our living room.

MOMMY
Were you in the living room when this occurred?

WOMAN
We were asleep. The crash woke us.

MOMMY
Eisa, wake up. We're home.

DIE

LARRY (GRANDMA)
The cinnamon rolls are ready.

MOMMY
Cinnamon rolls from Your Black Muslim Bakery!

EISA
I have a new stepfather. His name is Larry and he's a film-maker. I watch Kurosawa movies in his college course, Film and Social Change. He goes and gets ribs from Flint's BBQ even though we're vegetarian and he's not supposed to. His daughter Kafí moves into my room with me and there's a new feeling in the house: my mom doesn't seem to notice me anymore.

LARRY
Would you rather be a slave or die?

EISA
Larry is giving me my catechism. I don't like him. He doesn't pretend to be my father but who's that anyway?

LARRY
Slavery? Or death?

EISA
My catechism. (*to* LARRY) Um—neither.

LARRY
But if you were put in that position like our ancestors were, what would you do.

EISA
I don't know?

LARRY

If you had to choose, what would you do?

ANGELA

(*looking at* EISA) In *Back to the Future*, Michael J. Fox is in two places at once: the past and the future.

EISA

Right! To fix things! (*to* SELF) I guess I would want to live. Then I could learn to read and escape like Frederick Douglass. I could be a stop on the Underground Railroad! I could be like Harriet Tubman and lead people to freedom through the woods! (*to* LARRY) Be a slave?

LARRY

(*thundering*) NO!!!! No. You should DIE. You should choose death instead of slavery.

> EISA *reaches her hand out to* MOMMY.
> MOMMY *doesn't notice her.*

EISA

I never express my opinion in our house again.
(*quietly*) *Ohhhh, freedom.*
Ohhhh, freedom.
Ohhhh, freedom over me.
And before I'd be a slave
I'd be buried in my grave
And go home to my Lord and be free.

CHECKLIST

> MOMMY *is sitting at a table working.*
> EISA *tries to get her attention with the*
> *checklist.*

GRANDMA
matching iridescent Wet and Wild lipstick and nail polish (99
cents each or boosted from Kress)!

CHORUS (GRANDMA, CES, + EISA)
CHECK!

CES
Dr. Bronner's peppermint soap!

CHORUS
CHECK!

EISA
Egyptian Musk or China Rain perfume from the original
Body Shop on Telegraph Avenue!

CHORUS
CHECK!

GRANDMA
CP Shades overdyed jeans!

CHORUS
CHECK!

CES
Mia moccasins!

CHORUS
CHECK!

EISA
Levi's from Miller's Outpost!

CHORUS
CHECK!

GRANDMA
Indian Earth blush in hand thrown pot!

CHORUS
CHECK!

CES
silver hoop earrings!

CHORUS
CHECK!

EISA
silver rings!

CHORUS
CHECK!

GRANDMA
silver necklaces!

CHORUS
CHECK!

CES
no blood stained gold, platinum or diamonds from Sierra
Leone!

CHORUS
CHECK!

EISA
hair mousse!

CHORUS
CHECK!

GRANDMA
acid wash jean jacket AND matching pants!

CHORUS
CHECK!

CES
blow dried asymmetrical hair!

CHORUS
CHECK!

EISA
no need for peace button on backpack 'cause we talk and walk it everyday!

CHORUS
CHECK!

GRANDMA
backpack slung over one shoulder NOT both!

CHORUS
CHECK!

CES
no purse—too girly!

CHORUS
CHECK!

EISA
no allowance (parents have no money this month)!

CHORUS
CHECK!

GRANDMA
rennetless Monterey Jack cheese sandwich on 12 grain with
mustard, mayo, avocado and alfalfa sprouts!

CHORUS
CHECK!

CES
peanut butter, honey and banana on whole wheat!

CHORUS
CHECK!

EISA
agar agar all natural homemade jello!

CHORUS
CHECK!

GRANDMA
tempeh sticks!

CHORUS
CHECK!

CES
granola with yogurt!

CHORUS
CHECK!

EISA
yogurt with cinnamon and honey!

CHORUS
CHECK!

GRANDMA
hibiscus iced tea!

CHORUS
CHECK!

CES
unfiltered apple juice!

CHORUS
CHECK!

EISA
nothing, not even fries or apple pie from McDonalds, Burger King, or Wendy's!

CHORUS
CHECK!

GRANDMA
Kentucky Fried Chicken has rat tails in each bucket!

CHORUS
CHECK!

CES
butter—or Willow Run margarine—on everything!

CHORUS
CHECK!

> EISA, GRANDMA, *and* CES *collapse into laughter.* EISA *looks at* MOMMY *to* ANGELA.

PIANO

> ANGELA *plays some Saint-Saens on her clarinet.*

EISA
In the early '80s, Angela and I dressed exactly the same. We wore purple. Purple everything.

ANGELA + EISA
Check!

EISA
I played piano, and she played clarinet.
And this was before *Purple Rain.*

> *Shalamar's "This Is For The Lover In You" plays.*

The blind woman who lets me practice piano at her house has a daughter who is in a music school on the UC Berkeley campus. At age 10, I am accepted to the school, the Young Musicians Program. You have to be poor and talented to get in. This means there are lots of cute black boys! I love music and summer mornings. (*Shalamar out*) "*My kitty kat craves chicken, my kitty kat craves milk.*"

MOMMY
No singing commercials in the house!

MOMMY	EISA
No commercials! TV. The boob tube. All lies. They've got a TV show about SWAT. Glorifying SWAT. They invented SWAT to	"*My kitty cat craves tuna So my kitty kat craves Crave yeah my kitty kat craves Crave!*"

take down the Panthers.
They raided the office in LA
and even shot a black state
senator when he got in the
way. The pigs would break in
and put nails in our spaghetti.
Because, according to J. Edgar
Hoover, the Panthers were the
greatest threat to the internal
security of the country. After
what we lived through, you
think we can trust the media?
The government?

Let's get physical,
physical, I wanna get
physical, let's get
into physical
Let me hear your body
talk, your body talk, let me
hear your body
talk, oh let's get
animal, animal
I wanna get animal

EISA

I sneak it all anyway.
One morning, Larry makes me 12 pancakes. After that, I
really like him and laugh at all his jokes.
I listen to The Police on KROC.
And then this afternoon I'm playing Debussy,
on the 9-foot Steinway concert grand.
When the big oak doors to the stage open, you come out, play
music. And if they really like you, you can come out for a
second or third bow. I'm so glad to be playing this song.
I feel fresh from my shower
and I smell like this nice perfume.
I feel normal.
I have a crush on a boy.

ANGELA

When Eisa was little we put her into the tub with Kojo, the
son of one of the members of my legal team. And as soon as
she got into that tub, she saw his penis and grabbed it! He

screamed and screamed.

Everyone but EISA *laughs.*

EISA

(*whispers to* AUDIENCE) I have a crush on a boy. He plays oboe. I want to kiss him. I write his name in my diary every night Art Deco style, and then I kiss the page with my mint toothpaste lips. I call him on the phone and try to make him laugh. I do everything to make him notice me. He's Filipino and chubby and has black hair falling over his eyes. I love him and I love *Fame*. The movie and the TV show. I like the music and I have the record. I love Donna Summer and the working class people and the Soviet Union. And they open the doors.

EISA *goes to the piano.*

Debussy. C octave in the left hand.

EISA *plays Debussy's La Cathédral engloutie.*

GRENADA

EISA

I don't want to go to Grenada, Mom. I'll miss the final concert.

MOMMY

(*dismissive*) The whole family is going, Eisa. Not just the four of us, but Grandma, Angela, your godmother Fannie, your cousins—there's no question.

EISA
Can't I stay here?

MOMMY

You're coming with us. It's the first peaceful socialist revolution in a black country—it's a beacon of hope for all of us. It's beautiful there. The people are happy because they've overthrown their oppression. They are making their own country now.

EISA

I'm going to miss the final concert.

MOMMY

Eisa, you'll be there next year. Going to Grenada is a once in a lifetime opportunity to see the revolution in action.

EISA

(*stops playing; to* AUDIENCE) But what about my oboe player? He has big feelings. Sometimes he gets so frustrated with playing a piece in concert, he just walks off the stage. He crescendoes and decrescendoes real well. And his tone is so sweet and pure. Lionel Richie and Diana Ross have an oboe on "Endless Love." I write him a song.

EISA *plays and sings.*

Everyone can tell how I'm feeling
They know how I'm feeling
And everyone who knows how I'm feeling
Can see the pain in my eyes
All I know is that my world's fallin apart
Since I left you, oh no
That's the way my life goes by
Cute and brief, only flirtations
That's the way my life goes by
Are they meaningful—
or momentary fluctuations
I'm just looking for a special man to love

I need someone like you, ooh ooh ooh

> EISA *begins playing the Debussy again.*

MOMMY
(*impatient*) Are you trying to have a conversation with me?

EISA
(*to* AUDIENCE) We don't have conversations anymore. (*to*
MOMMY) Can't I stay?

MOMMY
You're going to Grenada.

EISA
And I go.

> EISA *stops playing and gets up from
> the piano. "Can't Stand Losing You"
> by The Police plays.*

Stopover in Barbados. The tiny plane we take, wallpapered
blue on the inside. Orange juice so sweet I can barely drink it.
As we land, we hit several trees. The runway is not very long
or paved.

CES
We drive to our house on the left side of a road shaded by
banana trees.

EISA
Ces! (*She hugs her.*) We can hang out, make up songs and
dances, watch TV.

CES
There's nothing on TV but local news and *Superman 2*.

> *"Wanted Dead or Alive" by Mighty
> Sparrow.*

The house we're staying in was built

EISA
by an eccentric man, we are told.

CES
You take your shower on the balcony,

EISA
without curtains, exposed and cold.

CES
You can see the sea everywhere you look

EISA
over the jungle leaves.

CES
There's a moth

EISA
the size of a bat

CES + EISA
hanging on our bunkbed sheet!

CES
My brother Benji gets diarrhea all over my bed. He laughs about it. My cousin Kafí gets hives from her mosquito bites. Aunt Fania steps on a sea urchin. We eat only bread and fruit juice for breakfast.

CES + EISA
We wanted Grandma's big Birmingham breakfasts—

EISA
grits,

CES
eggs,

EISA
bacon,

CES
fruit,

EISA
toast—

CES
But this is a continental breakfast,

EISA
we are told,

CES
so bread and juice

EISA
is all she wrote.

CES
Why is it called a continental breakfast
when continents are so big?
We run out of food toward the end of the trip, and Berna-
dette, a woman the Grenadians have hired to cook for us,
makes a decision. The rooster that wakes us every morning
with its crowing from the enclosed courtyard is gone one
night, and then served on our plates. He is thin and rawbony.
We are quiet at dinner as we eat the rooster we once knew.

EISA
We perform after dinner.

> EISA *and* CES *do the Smurf as they sing.*

CES + EISA
Don't. Dontchu want me.
You know I don't believe you
when you say that you don't need me.
Don't. Dontchu want me.

EISA
We eat a lot of mangoes and nutmeg. Our house is next door to the airport Cuba is helping Grenada build. It has a longer runway than the one where we landed in the trees.

"Yankees Gone" by Mighty Sparrow.

CES
The city is filled with hilly streets. Everyone seems so happy. We go into people's homes and everyone talks about life after the revolution. Life since the dictator, Gairy, had been thrown out. The prime minister Maurice Bishop and cabinet member Jacqueline Creft spend a lot of time with Angela and my aunt Fania talking about politics.

GRANDMA
As a reading specialist, I am helping the Grenadian government develop their primary education policy.

EISA
My godmother Fannie loves the island so much she decides she'll leave Oakland and move here with her two children, Damani and Kai.

I spend the night at the Coards'. They are in the government, the New Jewel Movement, and have two daughters. I make friends with the oldest girl, Shola, and lay on her bed reading her books in the yellow light through the curtain.

My hair is in cornrows that cross into two balls at the top of

my head. *Superman 2* becomes more and more philosophical
with each viewing. Should you give up your superpowers for
love or should you save the world?

MOMMY
This country is perfect. Black and socialist.

EISA
Flying home, we can see the black and white sand on the beach.
Death will visit.
President Ronald Reagan will invade.

ANGELA *plays her clarinet.*

REAGAN (GRANDMA)
(*speaking on TV*) Fidel Castro is building a military base
disguised as an airport!

EISA
(*talking back to the TV*) They need a new airport so we don't
land in the trees.

REAGAN
We will drive the Communists out.

EISA
Are you gonna do the same thing in Berkeley?

REAGAN
There has been a coup and we must invade to bring political
stability to the region.

MOMMY
Maurice Bishop has been killed. Jacqueline Creft has been killed.

EISA
Shola's family are the prime suspects. Are Fannie and Damani
and Kai safe?

REAGAN

We must save the American citizens enrolled in Grenada's medical school from the forces of evil.

EISA

We demonstrate in the streets of Berkeley the first night of the invasion. We already have a bumper sticker on our Honda Accord that says

CHORUS

U.S. OUT OF GRENADA.

REAGAN

We have victory in Grenada. Capitalism has been restored.

ANGELA *stops playing.*

EISA

(*desperate*) What happened? Who did we meet that summer who was infiltrating the government, secretly working for the CIA? Why couldn't the revolution last?

CHORUS

(*singing softly*) *let the rain come down*
let the rain come down
let the rain come down, down

I DON'T KNOW

EISA
Unzima lomthwalo ufuna madoda
Unzima lomthwalo ufuna bafazi.

CHORUS
Divest now! UC Berkeley out of South Africa!

Azikatani nomasiya boshwa sizi misel inkululeko.

EISA
(*speaking as the* CHORUS *continues to sing*) I've been cutting classes to protest the university's investments in the apartheid government and businesses of South Africa, and my mother is organizing a concert of freedom songs. (*singing with* CHORUS) *Azikatani nomasiya boshwa sizi misel inkululeko.*

She walks over to ANGELA'S *house.*

Angela's dog Amira has a litter of puppies. What a smell! Angela gives them all away and saves one for me. I name her Mariposa.

MOMMY
You didn't ask me about this first, Angela.

ANGELA
She wants the puppy. Why can't she have it?

MOMMY
You have more space up here. You have dog space, we have cat space.

ANGELA
Why don't you bring her home and then see?

MOMMY
It's a lot of responsibility, Eisa.

EISA
We bring Mariposa home and I teach her to sit on our back stairs. But when the sun sets, we take her back to Angela's. (*to* ANGELA) Mom says I can't keep her. You'll have to give her to someone else.

ANGELA
Eisa, have you ever seen a yellow watermelon before?

EISA
Yellow watermelon? You're teasing me.

ANGELA
This is one right here. Don't you believe me?

EISA
No. Watermelon is red.

ANGELA
Watch when I cut it.

She cuts it.

EISA
It's yellow!

ANGELA
See? What you expect and what you get aren't always the same. Amira needs some company. I'll keep Mariposa here for you when you visit.

EISA
Really?

ANGELA
Don't you believe me?

EISA
I believe you. Thanks.

> As EISA *starts to exit,* ANGELA *calls after her.*

ANGELA
And watermelon comes in all colors. Purple too.

MOMMY
Angela.

> ANGELA *laughs as* EISA *and* MOMMY
> *leave her house.*

MOMMY
(*to* EISA) Those jeans are so tight, I don't know how you sit.

EISA
(*playing Debussy's Sarabande from* Suite Pour le Piano) I
love the model Talisa Soto. To me she is incredibly beautiful
and mysterious. She only goes by her first name and is in all
the fashion magazines. My gym partners and I try to dress
like she does, wearing Ray Ban knockoffs and scarves draped
around our heads and necks on the racquetball court. I also
try to dress like the actress Dorothy Dandridge in a candid
shot of her at home—white polo shirt, jeans rolled up to the
knees, bandana worn as a belt, bitten apple in hand. Still, no
luck with boys.

Who's my real father? Did he do something wrong that got
passed on to me? I wish I could go back in time and fix the
future. The now.

Are relationships even allowed to work? Grandma and Papa
were together till he died. Uncle Ben and Aunt Sylvia, Ces's
parents, are forever too. But they don't live in California.
Everyone here is divorced. Everyone here has lovers or friends
or understandings or open relationships. All I know is my
mother and father broke up right after Angela was acquitted,
and my mother and stepfather will divorce my first year of
college. Angela is divorced too and many friends pass through
the house. But no one is sad. Everyone is optimistic. Maybe
this is the way things are supposed to be.

When I feel sad, I play piano or go over to Angela's house. Then I feel better.

THAT'S IT

> EISA *practices something hard and showy, maybe Rachmaninoff.*

STUDENT (CES)
Is your mom coming to the recital?

EISA
I don't know.

STUDENT
I've never met her. What's she like?

EISA
Tall.

STUDENT
That's hella stupid. For real though.

EISA
She's really busy so.

> *She plays the end chords from Debussy's Toccata from* Suite Pour le Piano *to finish the recital. She bows. Applause.*
>
> *Then she waits. And waits.*

TEACHER (GRANDMA)
Do you need a ride home?

EISA
If it's no problem.

TEACHER
You did well. You're finally playing the piano instead of letting the piano play you.

EISA + CES
Duh nuh nuh nuh nuh nuh nuh nuh
Duh nuh nuh nuh nuh
Yeah yeah
Computer blue

LARRY (GRANDMA)
Fania, end of discussion.

MOMMY
No, I haven't finished my thought yet—

LARRY
End of discussion.

MOMMY
I don't know where that came from but don't say that to me.

EISA
Larry and my mom are arguing at an Ethiopian restaurant. I am as quiet as a napkin. We go out to the car in the dark parking lot and they drive off without me.

> *Lights go out. Complete darkness.*

EISA
I'm here! I exist!

> *Eventually there is the sound of a car screeching around the corner. Lights come back up.*

EISA
How could you leave me?

MOMMY
Well if you want to get into the car, you should be more aggressive!

EISA
(*furious*) That's it. Me and Mom are over.

OOPS

> *The tape in the boombox clicks off, and the red light goes out.*

CES
(*to* EISA) Tape stopped. (*to* AUDIENCE) Gotta flip it over, old school.

EISA
(*to* CES) Wind it past the leader—the white part before the brown tape—

CES
I know, with my pinkie—

EISA
(*covering, to* AUDIENCE) Ces is Angela's niece too. How do you feel when—

CES
Wait, it's not on yet.

EISA
Actually, that's okay. We're getting to the part where I com-

mit high treason against the Davises and betray the race.

CES
It's easy to do.

EISA
You never did that.

CES
I grew up in Cleveland. I don't have her name. Go ahead.

EISA
It's on?

CES
Angela's Mixtape, y'all.

MIXED

QUINTESSA (CES)
"Are you mixed?"

EISA
asked Quintessa, a black girl at my junior high.

"King of Pain" by The Police.

CES
Back it up: Aunt Fania is trying to give Eisa the perfect education.

GRANDMA
Education is the key to progress.

CES
First there was the diverse but so-so grammar school. Then

the excellent but all white and rich elementary school.

MOMMY
Wait. There were also Asian students.

CES
But their parents have just as much money.

EISA
I hate the homemade looking clothes my mother dresses me in. I would walk out the door in the lederhosen she'd brought me from her last trip to the Eastern bloc, then change into jeans and sneakers behind the trash bins.

ANGELA
"In 1970, my young bodyguard Jonathan Jackson publishes an article in the student newspaper he co-edits.

'I am the only Black in my English, U.S. History and Algebra II classes, and one of three in my chemistry class...I am constantly being bombarded with such questions as: "Where did you learn that?" and "Where did you get all this culture?"'"

POOR KID (GRANDMA)
Everyone is white or Asian and rich and lives in the Oakland hills. If you are black, you are poor and live in the flatlands. If you are black, you take another bus. Us black kids stand outside 7 Eleven and buy Jolly Ranchers and Coke flavored Slurpees and wait for the 59 bus. The white driver sees a bunch of black kids waiting to board and passes right by. We sometimes have to wait an entire hour before a bus driver decides to stop, before he decides we too have the right to go home.

EISA
My mother complains to the bus company,

MOMMY
but the bus drivers keep passing the black students up.

EISA
She makes me write an epic poem about the struggle of black people through history in response.

ANGELA
Eisa wrote a poem. Listen to this part.

"Pork and cornpone
Cornpone and pork
The slaves very much wished
They lived in New York
For there you were free
For there you were free"

EISA
Suddenly I don't want to be poor and my hair doesn't feather. I'm nothing at home and now I'm nothing at school.

RICH KID (CES)
Why are you crying?

EISA
(*crying*) I'm crying in the middle of PE.

RICH KID (CES)
What's wrong?

EISA
She has feathered hair and a huge house and make out parties.

RICH KID
What's the matter?

EISA
My mom doesn't like me? How do I say that?

RICH KID
It's okay. Let's go do cherry drops off the bars!

MOMMY
Eisa, get up. (EISA *does not move.*) Get up. (EISA *slowly sits up.*) There's a conference to establish an Economic Bill of Rights for all citizens. Food, housing, and employment are our natural born rights. We weren't put on this earth to dangle in some profiteering corporate scheme. At the plenary session, you'll do your Angela monologues again.

EISA
I never read the book. I just do the monologues. (*child acting again*) "In September 1949, I enrolled at Carrie A. Tuggle School. Many of the children there could not even afford to buy a bag of potato chips for lunch."

EISA + ANGELA
"It was agonizing for me to see some of my closest friends waiting outside the lunchroom silently watching the other children eating."

ANGELA
"Finally I decided to do something about it. Knowing that my father returned from his service station each evening with a bag of coins, which he left overnight in a kitchen cabinet, one night I stayed awake until the whole house was sleeping. Then, trying to overcome my deep fear of the dark, I slipped into the kitchen and stole some of the coins. The next day I gave the money to my hungry friends. Their hunger pangs were more compelling than my pangs of conscience."

EISA + ANGELA
"It seemed to me that if there were hungry children, something was wrong and if I did nothing about it, I would be

wrong too."

> EISA *forgets to bow.* CHORUS *applauds*
> *to cue her.* EISA *remembers, and bows.*

CHORUS
(*chanting*) El pueblo unido
jamás será vencido
The people united
will never be defeated

RICH KID
We get a new teacher this fall and everything changes. She has
a Russian name and big thighs and clogs and hair. She swims
eight miles a day. I think she's Jewish like me.

EISA
(*with a new energy*) My new teacher tells me I can't take
constructive criticism and this does it. I am tired of crying. I
begin to write stories. I read them out loud. My teacher and
the white kids love them so much I write sequels and read
them at recess. I am the entertainer. I am the leader. I now
have crew. We call ourselves the Room 1 Originals, because
everyone copies us. (*singing*) *How funky is your chicken*

CHORUS
How funky is your chicken

EISA
How loose is your goose

CHORUS
How loose is your goose

> EISA *drops to the floor, making things.*

MOMMY
You seem productive.

85

EISA

I am always on my floor making things. I am the saddest, happiest, and most creative I have ever been.

POOR KID

Wow, is that a vending machine that sells homemade stickers?

EISA

I don't tell anyone, but I am also trying to come up with an alternative utopic society.

POOR KID

And you made the vending machine out of a shoebox?

EISA

I want to create something important, a new ideology, a philosophical and economic system that does not have the pitfalls that socialism and capitalism seem to.

MOMMY

But you don't have enough black friends.

EISA

(*here it goes*) I don't. My closest friend is mixed.

MIXED FRIEND (CES)

My father is black, my mother is white, and we live in the hills.

> MIXED FRIEND *sings "We Are Family"*
> *under* EISA's *monologue.*

EISA

There are four other black girls in my class, but I don't like them. Three are too quiet, and one is too loud. The loud one has meningitis and the biggest titties of anyone in school. I go to her house a few times and listen to Sister Sledge but we don't really click. And there is Lamar, the black boy with green eyes. I really like him and don't realize it. He smells sweaty and I'm scared of him. He acts real crazy on the bus and is probably the reason the driver passes us. It's easier to like the white boys, 'cause I know they won't like me. But if I like Lamar, something may HAPPEN. "Me / the Rox / give up / the box?"

MOMMY
For 7th grade, you're going to a better school.

EISA
Where I have no friends. Public junior high. In Berkeley.

CES
There are more black kids there and the schooling is good.

CES + MOMMY
Perfect.

QUINTESSA (CES)
Are you mixed?

EISA
Quintessa asks me in gym class. This meant one black parent, one anything else. There are so many mixed kids in Berkeley, this is a legitimate question. If you are mixed, you don't have to follow the same rules. You can hang with anybody of any race—doesn't matter. Whoever. But if you were just black like me and hung with everybody, you'd get talked about to your face.

MOMMY
You don't have enough black friends.

EISA
I tried to calculate. My grandparents are both mixed, which makes Angela and my mom half white by blood, and I don't

know my dad. What does he even look like? He's black, but how black? I'm at least one quarter white. And someone probably raped someone on my dad's side—so maybe—

QUINTESSA
You mixed?

EISA
In science class, there's a mixed girl who decides that I should be her best friend.

MIXED FRIEND TWO (CES)
Wanna "crash" at my "pad"?

> MIXED FRIEND TWO *sings "Sweet Dreams (Are Made Of This)" by the Eurythmics under* EISA's *monologue.*

EISA
I accept. I think that being mixed means freedom. For her it means everything but. She feels she has to choose between black and white and doesn't want to. So she has all Asian friends instead. And me. We play handball with a Vietnamese girl named Ha.

But by high school, she's exchanged her Asian friends for all black ones, and I don't make the cut.

MIXED FRIEND TWO
You act like you're rich.

EISA
She didn't know me when I was handing red and brown food stamps to the cashier at The Co-op grocery store. But now that she's not super into school anymore like I am, I guess she doesn't make my cut either.

(*to* TEACHER) Can I do a presentation?

TEACHER (GRANDMA)
Fine. Class, Eisa is going to do a presentation for us.

EISA
This is something I've been working on that I want to share
with all of you. Broomstick, record player, and go.

> EISA *performs her "Dream" solo from*
> Flashdance. *At first quiet, unmoving,*
> *shy...*

He doesn't mean a thing to me
Just another purty face to see
He's all over town, knockin em down but honey
I'd never let him next to me

> *Then she lets it rip.*

Mmhm there he stares
Ask me if I care
Look he's comin closer hot damn I swear
He's got to be the toughest guy I've ever seen
I can't believe he's lookin at me
He's a a a ooh
He's a dream
(*shy again*) Thank you.

> EISA *finishes off with a quick Michael*
> *Jackson pencil turn, spinning at least*
> *twice.*

QUINTESSA
That was a cool song. Are you mixed?

EISA
Um—

MOMMY
Eisa, time to do your Angela monologues. We're protesting nuclear proliferation! That movie *War Games* was so inspiring.

ANGELA
(*begins*) "My sister Fania and I were walking—"

> *She looks at* EISA *to speak with her.*
> EISA *joins in as* YOUNG ANGELA.

EISA + ANGELA
"My sister Fania and I were walking in downtown Birmingham when I spontaneously proposed a plan to her: We would pretend to be foreigners and,"

> CES *joins in as* YOUNG FANIA.

EISA, ANGELA, + CES
"speaking French to each other, we would walk into the shoe store on 19th Street and ask, with a thick accent, to see a pair of shoes."

MANAGER (GRANDMA)
Can we help you?

CES
(*speaks French sounding gibberish*)

MANAGER
(*speaking slowly and enunciating*) I don't understand. Why don't you sit down.

EISA
"We were invited to take seats in the very front of this Jim Crow shop."

MANAGER
Now, what can I do for you pretty young ladies?

CES
(*silent*)

MANAGER
Where are you from?

CES
Quoi?

MANAGER
That's wonderful. And what on earth has brought you to a
place like Birmingham, Alabama? It's very seldom we get to
meet people like you, you know. Well—can I get you a shoe?

CES + EISA
(*gibberish and laughter*)

MANAGER
(*laughing*) Oh, I just never learned that language, forgive me,
we're simple people round here.

CES + EISA
(*more laughter*)

MANAGER
Is something funny?

CES + EISA
Oui.

MANAGER
What?

EISA
"All we have to do is pretend we're from another country and
you treat us like dignitaries."

CES
"Cracker!"

EISA bows quickly. CHORUS claps.

MOMMY
Why didn't you use the real French? I told you what we said.

*MOMMY sighs. EISA tries to exit, but
QUINTESSA stops her.*

QUINTESSA
You mixed? Or are you just (*she mimes opening an Oreo
cookie and licking the frosting off*). You know what kind of
cookie I'm talking about!

EISA
Why?

QUINTESSA
Because your skin is yellow
White girls who pass you in the hall always say hello*
You carry your books like they mean something to you
You ain't got a perm and your hair looks through
You be walking home a totally different direction
What math class you in? Cuz you ain't in my section
Oh, you be up in algebra balancin out equations
Then solve for x.

EISA
Y?

---

*   Alt lyric:
Because your skin's got something in it
White girls who pass you always stop and talk a minute

QUINTESSA
Cuz we're carvin up nations.
Black, white, Asian, Chicano
Everybody's representin, we ain't got no squabble
We just want to know which box you check
You check other, you're mixed, and there's no wreck to catch
You can flow interstate like a parasite or virus
You can hang with whoever and you won't have to fight us
You think you so cute and we think you cute too
But if you ain't got your biracial license—

EISA
I do.

QUINTESSA
You mixed?

INSULTS

MOMMY
You don't have enough black friends.

QUINTESSA (CES)
Do you know who you're talking to?

GRANDMA
You need to go to church.

MIXED FRIEND TWO (CES)
You act like you're rich.

LARRY (GRANDMA)
(*laughing*) It's the whitification of Eisa Davis.

QUINTESSA (CES)
Are you mixed?

LARRY
She's been whitified!

MOMMY
Let's see your report card. Alright, let's bring that one B up.

HALLWAY GIRL ONE (GRANDMA)
Bitch! Think you all that.

HALLWAY GIRL TWO (CES)
You trying to take my boyfriend?

STUDENT DIRECTOR (GRANDMA)
You gave the best audition, but you're black so I'm not calling you back for the part.

BLACKULA (CES)
You're Angela Davis's niece and I'm more political than you!

MOMMY
You think you're gonna play music and do plays all your life? That's not a career.

GRANDMA
You need to go to church. Give your talent to the Lord.

MOMMY
You don't have enough black friends. Angela and I went to white schools and we didn't have any problems.

QUINTESSA
You mixed?

A pause of epic proportion.

EISA
(*caving in*) Sure yeah.

QUINTESSA
You're mixed,

EISA
Mm hm.

QUINTESSA
(*a moment, then*) She's mixed y'all. Free pass. But you still need a perm though, 'cause your hair did not make it to the other side.

EISA + ANGELA
I am Angela Davis.

CHECKLIST PART 2

This checklist is bitter, angrier.

EISA
sneak two packs of Sugar Babies a day

CHORUS
check.

GRANDMA
sneak cheeseburger fries and apple pie for $1.63 at Mickey D's

CHORUS
check.

CES
sneak beef and bean burrito and glazed cinnamon roll from snack bar

CHORUS
check.

EISA
zits.

CHORUS
check.

GRANDMA
apply curling iron to bangs that revert in morning fog.

CHORUS
check.

CES
huge t shirt to hide hairy arms and high butt.

CHORUS
check.

EISA
watch everyone else play quarters, get drunk, make out.

CHORUS
check.

GRANDMA
see how long you can let the perm burn your scalp.

CHORUS
check.

CES
count scabs on scalp from perm touch up.

CHORUS
check.

EISA
big eyes.

CHORUS
check.

GRANDMA
mouth shut.

CHORUS
check.
hope. check.

I'M MAD

EISA
I smell like a white boy.
I work at it.
I'm always mad at home.
There's no space for me.

MOMMY
Eisa, play piano for the guests.

EISA
I'm doing my homework.

> We hear Elvis Costello's "Black and
> White World".

In high school, I wear glasses and sweatshirts, Hemingway,
Faulkner, and Fitzgerald.
Shorts and hightops, Trig and Physics.
Blazers if I'm debating or going to moot court.
Before the perm, my hair looks like a young animal still trying

to coordinate its limbs.
After the perm, it looks like it's been badly hurt in a fight.
I always keep it in a bun.
A boy told me it looked like a braided piece of shit.

MOMMY
You know Spanish, speak to the guests in it. They're from
Argentina.

EISA
I'm listening to Elvis Costello, Mom.
And Mozart. And Fauré.
Music is my refuge.
Libera me domine de morte eternam.

MUSIC TEACHER (GRANDMA)
(*overlapping the above at "de morte eternam"*)
Free me Lord, from eternal death.

EISA
We have moved up to the hills, but it's too late.
Now I want to live Southside in the flatlands like we used to.
I never live near my friends.

MOMMY
Toni Morrison is here for dinner, Eisa, come to the table!

EISA
I'm BUSY, Mom!
I've read *The Bluest Eye* and it was sad, but I am studying
whiteness. Learning it carefully.
Almost every day my friends and I exchange notes. Occa-
sionally we give mixtapes. On theirs are Prince and NWA,
Joni Mitchell and KRS-One. I make one that includes "Die
Nigga," by the Last Poets. My white friends love it.

GRANDMA

(*to* TONI, *played by* CES) You've always got to do your best or your first impression could be your last. I started Eisa reading and writing at age 2. First word she read was STOP.

MOMMY

(*to* TONI) But the first word she spoke. LIGHT.

GRANDMA

I insisted that all my children and all my grands would observe an hour of silent reading time every day after lunch. I won't leave this earth until all my grands are in college.

EISA

I don't know any other black kids who like books who I like. I don't want to look in the mirror.

EISA *suddenly looks to* ANGELA.

I write my college essays in Angela's kitchen.

ANGELA

(*looking at* EISA*'s essays*) I remember when I used to write like this. Convoluted, serpentine, endless sentences.

EISA

She keeps old jewelry in file boxes above the washer and dryer. I take a few stone rings she no longer wears.

HARVARD

MOMMY

Harvard? You'll need some training before you go. It's the citadel of capitalism, the bastion of elitism. I don't want you to be brainwashed, so Angela is going to give you a private tutorial in Marxism before you go. You'll have your communist principles from the source. Angela? Once a week. Start her on the early philosophical writings and then the *Manifesto*. Sections of *Kapital* as you see fit.

ANGELA
(*impatient*) You have to let the clutch out at the same time that you press the gas in.

EISA
(*to* AUDIENCE) Now that I've finished my Marxism primer, Angela is teaching me to drive a stick shift in her Nissan 300ZX.

ANGELA
Try it now.

EISA
I stall in front of a ranch house.

ANGELA
No, that's not it. You're going to strip the gears and burn out the clutch! Start the car. No, you have to leave the clutch in when you turn the key. Remember to put the gas in before you let the clutch out all the way. Don't ride it—

EISA
This is harder than Marx.

ANGELA
"The philosophers have only interpreted the world; the point, however, is to change it." Now let's see if you can put the car in second.

EISA *hugs her family goodbye.*

EISA
Bye Larry. Bye Kafi. Bye Angela.

My mother insists on packing all my things for me. (*getting into car*) Then something happens on our way to the airport. In the car, my mom reaches for my hand. (MOMMY *reaches for* EISA's *hand.*) Is she actually sad that I'm leaving? I don't get it. I pull my hand away to scratch my scalp in a place where it doesn't itch.

> ROOMMATE *and* EISA *drink beer.*

ROOMMATE (CES)
So you're from Berkeley?

EISA
Yeah. And Oakland. They're right next to each other but different. Berkeley has professors and a park named after Ho Chi Minh. Oakland has lower rents and crack.

ROOMMATE
And you're Angela Davis's daughter? What was that like?

EISA
I'm actually her niece. (*to* AUDIENCE) But I feel like her daughter.

> MOMMY *reaches out her hand to* EISA.
> EISA *ignores her. De La Soul's "Three Is The Magic Number" plays.*

EISA
I ignore my mother but use her credit card. I find my father's address and start writing him letters he never responds to. I lose my virginity to a white boy I meet in a chemistry placement exam. My mom and Larry get a divorce and a month later Mr. Chemistry breaks up with me.

Without realizing it, I've begun to read the same German philosophers that Angela studied with in school. Books that are only in print today because Angela and other students retyped, mimeographed, and smuggled those manuscripts from Europe into the States. Angela told me to read the book about her life, and finally, on my first visit to New York City, I do.

> EISA *pulls out Angela's autobiography as she and* CES *sing one phrase of the "On Broadway" bassline.*

She sends me an allowance and writes me a letter every month. I'm starting to understand who she is to the world.

FREE ANGELA

> EISA *reads the book.*

EISA
While a professor of philosophy at UCLA, Angela was fighting to free George Jackson and the Soledad Brothers. At age 18, George had been sent to prison for sitting in the car of an acquaintance who took $70 from a service station. His sentence? One year to life. Now he was 28. Ten years for $70?

CHORUS
August 7th, 1970.

> EISA *puts on "Free Angela" by Bayete. The actors speak with urgency: they are speaking publicly to save* ANGELA's *life.*

MOMMY

Seventeen-year-old Jonathan Jackson walked into the Marin County Courthouse with Angela's gun and took hostages, including the judge and DA. He wanted to liberate his brother George and all political prisoners. The sheriffs murdered Jonathan in the parking lot. They called it a shoot out, but it was a shoot IN. They shot into Jonathan's van and he never shot out. Those pigs even murdered their own judge. Jonathan never fired a single shot.

LAWYER (CES)

(a speech) Angela Davis had nothing whatsoever to do with the Slave Insurrection of August 7th, 1970.

MOMMY

I am in Los Angeles en route to Cuba the night of

CHORUS

August 7th, 1970.

MOMMY

I have conceived a child.

EISA

I am conceived in Los Angeles on August 7th, 1970, the eve of my mother's 23rd birthday. I am conceived the night of the Marin County Courthouse rebellion.

CHORUS

October 13th, 1970.

EISA

Angela is arrested at Howard Johnson's on 8th Avenue in New York City, and taken to the Women's House of Detention in her disguise of dark glasses and straight hair.

CHORUS
October 13th, 1970.

LAWYER
New York State has put Angela in 4B, the cellblock for mental patients.

MOMMY
Who is crazy, her or her jailers?

LAWYER
Angela is locked in a barren, sunless cell soon to stand trial for her life on charges that she kidnapped, murdered and conspired with seventeen-year-old Jonathan Jackson to commit those crimes and to secure the rescue and escape of his brother, George Jackson, and the brothers in Soledad.

EISA
I am in utero, floating in a perfect amniotic heaven—and Angela is imprisoned, in the cárcel, incarcerated.

MOMMY
Prisoners are often murdered and they'll call it suicide. Free my sister!

LAWYER + MOMMY + GRANDMA
(*with black power salute*) Free Angela!

MOMMY
(*a speech*) Free Angela and all political prisoners! This is a mass movement. She was fired from her job at UCLA by Governor Ronald Reagan because she is a revolutionary. Because she is fighting for the liberation of all oppressed peoples!

GRANDMA
Jonathan Jackson, the seventeen-year-old brother of political prisoner George Jackson, took a gun Angela kept for

her protection without her knowledge. As an activist and a Communist, she received death threats every day. One of her bodyguards was

GRANDMA + EISA
Jonathan Jackson

EISA

who wanted his brother's freedom just as Angela did. Jonathan who was shot dead, but never fired a single shot.

LAWYER
Because Jonathan is already dead, they need a scapegoat for the public.

MOMMY
It was Angela's gun. She goes underground.

FISA

And she is arrested and brought to the Women's House of Detention. (*prison doors slam*) When I am born, Angela is still in jail.

ANGELA

Even on the day Eisa is born, my sister Fania spends a few hours at the jail with me. It is May 5th, Cinco de Mayo, Karl Marx's birthday.

EISA
People all over the country are raising money to free Angela.

> "Sweet Black Angel" by the Rolling Stones plays.

MOTHER IN IOWA (GRANDMA)
Save our sister! Knishes for Angela!

EISA
Aretha Franklin says she will post bail.

ARETHA (CES)
"Angela Davis must go free. Black people will be free. I've been locked up (for disturbing the peace in Detroit) and I know you've got to disturb the peace when you can't get no peace. Jail is hell to be in. I'm going to see her free if there is any justice in our courts, not because I believe in communism but because she's a Black woman and she wants freedom for Black people. I have the money; I got it from Black people—they've made me financially able to have it, and I want to use it in ways that will help our people."

EISA
People all over the world want Angela free.

RUSSIAN CHILD IN RED SCARF HOLDING ROSE (GRANDMA)
A million roses for Angela!

EISA + CES
August 21st, 1971.

EISA + CES + GRANDMA
August 21st, 1971.

CHORUS (ALL)
August 21st, 1971.

MOMMY
(*anguished*) George Jackson has been murdered in cold blood by prison guards.

Silence.

CHORUS
Free all political prisoners!

MOMMY

My name is Fania Davis. I have traveled around the world
and everyone knows that George was innocent. That Angela
has been imprisoned for 16 months on charges of which she
is entirely innocent! So who's guilty? J. Edgar Hoover, and
Ronald Reagan, and the systematic racist practices of the red
white and blue! I weaned my own child at two months and
left her with my mother in Birmingham to come here and
speak to you, to save my sister's life.

GRANDMA

My name is Sallye Davis. I am Angela's and Fania's mother.
I am Ben's and Reggie's mother. I am Eisa's and Cecilie's and
Benji's grandmother. I also speak publicly on Angela's behalf.
I hold Eisa in one arm and make the Black Power salute with
the other.

CHORUS

June 4th, 1972.

EISA

Angela is acquitted of all charges.

I never knew this. New knowledge, new gratitude.

> MOMMY *reaches her hand out to* EISA.

MOMMY

Eisa, let's go to the ashram and chant. Gurumayi is doing dar-
shan. Don't you want some shaktipat? (*singing*) *Om ganesha
ya namaha.*

EISA

The Berlin Wall has fallen, the Soviet Union has collapsed,
and Angela and my mother leave the Communist Party. My
mom cuts her hair off and gets braces. She goes on fasts in

which she drinks only cayenne pepper maple syrup lemonade.
She prays and chants and meditates. I continue to avoid her.
Angela comes to speak at Harvard.

ANGELA
"When Malcolm X came to speak, I was one of only five or
six black students at my college. This was the moment when I
first felt the stirrings of 'nationalism' in my—as I might have
articulated it then—'Negro Soul.' I felt empowered. I felt
extremely good. I might even say I experienced joy."

EISA	ANGELA
After I heard Angela speak,	"After I heard Malcolm X speak,"

ANGELA + EISA
"I was able to construct a psychological space within which I
could celebrate my body, my musical proclivities, my sup-
pressed speech patterns. As a result, I felt a strengthening of
ties with the community of my birth."

> *Applause. We hear "Eric B for Presi-*
> *dent" by Eric B and Rakim.*

ANGELA
I'm interviewing Ice Cube. Would you like to be my hip hop
consultant?

EISA
Hip hop is at the peak of its political consciousness and
now everybody's bringing music and activism together. Now
they're one and the same.

> *"Eric B for President" blends into*
> *Public Enemy's "Fight the Power."*

MOMMY
(*to self*) If only I could dance all day. (*cheery*) What are the
newest dances, Eisa?

> EISA *dances like Rosie Perez in the
> opening to* Do The Right Thing.

ANGELA
Do you want to go have Thai food with Toni? She said you
were busy doing homework the last time she came by.

EISA
Thank God, a second chance with Toni Morrison!

ANGELA
Eisa, do you want to go see Queen Latifah for New Year's Eve?

EISA
I just met her at school! She put footage of you in her video.
And Chuck D and Public Enemy just came to campus. We
had a roundtable on misogyny.

ANGELA
I saw myself in their video too.

> *The roundtable. Music out.*

EISA
When we women point to the ways in which your songs
"She Watch Channel Zero" and "Sophisticated Bitch" simply
replay the hegemonic culture you claim to subvert, it is not
to undermine or emasculate but to reveal how your internal-
ized racism finds expression as sexism, as hatred toward your
female counterparts.

CHUCK D (GRANDMA)
Hunh. I never thought about it like that.

FLAV (CES)
Yeah boyyyyyyyy!

> *Queen Latifah's "Wrath of My Madness".*

ANGELA
"Today, of course, young people are explicitly inspired by
what they know about Malcolm X and the Black Panther
Party. And I find myself in a somewhat problematic position because my own image appears now and then in visual
evocations of this nationalist impulse that fuel the advocacy
of revolutionary change in contemporary hip hop culture.
These days, young people who were not even born when I
was arrested often approach me with expressions of awe and
disbelief. On the one hand, it is inspiring to discover a mea-
sure of historical awareness that, in our youth, my generation
often lacked. But it is also unsettling. Because I know that
almost inevitably my image is associated with a certain repre-
sentation of Black nationalism that privileges those particular
nationalisms with which some of us were locked in constant
battle."

AFRICA

PORTER
Name?

EISA
Angela Eisa Davis on the 9 o'clock flight to Dakar.

> *We hear Youssou N'Dour's "Tan Bi".*
> *Lights are the warm sun of Senegal.*

EISA
Africa! I always wanted to come here. Black people run
everything!

ANGELA
Say "motherland" for the camera. Say "Africa!" the tour
guide says.

EISA
Amazing how those words will make you smile.
Africa is big. Why'd we come to Senegal?

ANGELA
Guess.

EISA
Why?

ANGELA
It's the cheapest package we could find.

EISA
Is our family from here?

ANGELA
Somewhere around here. Most slaves were taken from this
part of Africa.

EISA
Why did the child in the Mandinka village think we were
white people? Too bop! she screamed, and ran away.

ANGELA
Mixing.

EISA
Senegalese children beg us, the descendants of slaves, for
money. We have more because our ancestors were enslaved.

We walk out of the slavehouse. A vendor tells us not to cry. It's just history, he says. It's all over.

ANGELA
We see Fulani women pounding rice—it sounds like a symphony.

EISA
Swimming in the most perfect ocean water I have ever felt.

ANGELA
Divers jumping off the Gorée Island ferry after coins people throw into the water. They come up with the coins in their mouths.

EISA
Africa. I don't want to leave. Here, nothing separates me from myself.

Music out.

When I come back to the States, I stop perming my hair and get it braided. I fall in love with a black man, with blackness. And if you're not black—I'm still your friend.

CES
Hey.

EISA
What?

CES
I think you forgot something.

CES *points to* MOMMY *praying.*

THEY SHOOTIN'

EISA *reluctantly walks to* MOMMY. *She sprinkles snuff and turns to* EISA.

MOMMY
(*a prayer*) Thank you thank you with all my heart and spirit o ancestors, thank you for bringing us the fruits of the day.
I give you my food, Yemoja, Oshun, sweet honey for you Oshun, to ask that you bless my child with happiness and love to fulfill every aspect of her being.
Great orishas, hear me. Take this snuff as an offering of my gratitude for this moment and all the others to come.

CES + EISA
(*sings*)
Yemoja assessu, assessu
Yemoja
Yemoja assessu, assessu
Yemoja
Yemoja olodo, olodo Yemoja
Yemoja olodo, olodo Yemoja

MOMMY
Graduation! I'm going to invite your father. You know you are graduating from college on the 20th anniversary of Angela's acquittal?

EISA
My father? But I don't know him.

MOMMY
You are so much alike. You have his forehead, scrunched up little brow. Always independent, taking everything so seriously. Like with your music. How you practice all day sometimes.

EISA
But it's not a career.

MOMMY
What do you mean? I wish I were in the arts.

EISA
That's new. Goes with the braces.

MOMMY
Why are you so angry with me?

EISA
You mean you want my opinion? I was never allowed to
have one in the house. Whenever I showed any courage you
stamped it out.

MOMMY
Well I'm sorry I didn't give you what you needed. It just
seemed like you raised yourself. I don't know how you
became the person you are.

EISA
If I raised myself, I must be his child not yours. I could never
do anything right for you, so I try to be like whoever he is
and disappear.

MOMMY
No, no.

EISA
Yes. You don't care about me. You just tell me what to do.
I don't know who you are. No feelings are allowed in this
house.

MOMMY
Everything's just so different now. After perestroika, the Soviet

coup, the divorce... I'm tired of fighting. I'm still in the struggle, but there's got to be another way. (*pause*) Eisa. I'm sorry.

EISA
I don't know where I come from—

MOMMY
Yes you do.

EISA
Then who's my father?

MOMMY
(*surprised*) You don't know?

EISA
You never said anything.

MOMMY
You were there.

EISA
In your uterus.

MOMMY
Well, it was the movement. The struggle. No one ever laughed, we were at war. Your father, so eloquent. I just fell for that. Beautiful man, big arms, handsome. We were in the struggle together—and I was struggling against him. I took my marriage vows seriously, but he was beating me. After a while, I just didn't feel love anymore. I started coming into my woman's consciousness. Started taking karate to protect myself from him. Then he started to take it too.

EISA
He hit you?

MOMMY
You should get to know him. He's in DC.

EISA
I know where he is, Mama. There's more. Tell me.

MOMMY
Being with me wasn't easy on him either.

EISA
Why?

MOMMY
It was the struggle. Everything happening with Angela...
Before Jonathan was killed, before Angela went underground,
when your father and I were also graduate students in philosophy, we were staying in the apartment Angela kept near school.

Reagan had just fired her from UCLA.
One night your father and I had a fight.

EISA
You had a fight.

MOMMY
I ran out of the house barefoot.
The pigs were there casing the place.
They followed me.
"Are you Angela Davis?" they asked.

EISA
"Are you Angela Davis?"

MOMMY
I said, "Pig, get out of my face!"
But those cops kept following me.
Your father saw the altercation and came outside.

The pigs pulled their guns on him.
Your father had his gun inside the house and he went to go get it.

EISA
And the pigs followed him

MOMMY
And I pulled on their arms trying to stop them.
But they got in the house and they shot your father.
I grabbed the pig's arm and the rest of the bullets emptied out
into the walls and ceiling. But your father had his shotgun
and fought back, ran them out the house.
We got him to the hospital.
And by the time I came back and called Angela, the pigs
showed up and arrested me. They even pointed a rifle at our
neighbors' baby.
Your father had been shot in the shoulder.
The bullet lodged just a quarter of an inch from his spine.
But they got it out, and then they threw him in jail.
The charge was attempted murder of a peace officer.

EISA
I barely got born.

MOMMY
Born of the blood of the struggle. We fought to have the
charges dropped. He was released and we made you, our
beautiful, perfect daughter. The day you were born, I brought
you to visit Angela in jail. The matron told me that I couldn't
bring you in, that I should know jail is no place for babies.
I told her well it's no place for my sister either. Jonathan
Jackson died for his brother. He laid down his life to liberate
his brother George from his chains. I am Angela's sister and if
necessary, I will do the same.

EISA *takes* MOMMY's *hand.*

EISA

(*to* AUDIENCE) Will I? Would I rather be a slave or die?
How must I spend my life to meet my family's eye?
As an out of work actress I used to waitress across the street
from where the Women's House of Detention stood.
In grad school, I wrote plays in the library there—a library
that may once have been Angela's in prison.
I still sing freedom songs but at nightclubs instead of demon-
strations.

"Chisa" by Abdullah Ibrahim plays.

EISA
Am I living up to my name?

ANGELA
So this mixtape wasn't for me at all.

EISA
Of course it is. I just don't know if you like it.

ANGELA
Autobiography doesn't define you. How you see the world
does. Like in Birmingham, Mother or Daddy picked up my
books downtown, or else the black librarian, Miss Bell,
would bring them by the house.

EISA
Ces and I went to the library with Miss Bell in the summer-
time too.

ANGELA
She was Alma Powell's aunt you know. Alma who married
Colin Powell. Mother went to their wedding.

EISA
You grew up with her?

ANGELA
Yup. Her and Condoleezza. But she was younger. We all went to the same library.

Remember when you sent me your undergraduate thesis paper, and you were writing about *In Living Color*? About laughter and the role of parody in resistance and how meaning changes when private utterances like playing the dozens become popular entertainment that may actually coincide with and reproduce racist and sexist representations? How the whole of popular culture in America is based upon the minstrel show? I liked it. You told me you didn't, that it wasn't exactly how you wanted to do it. I told you to revise it, to keep working. That was something you hadn't even thought of. You just wanted to give up.

EISA
The strength you all have—I just don't have it. I honestly don't know if I belong in this family.

ANGELA
You're the only one who's ever thought that. What, you want me to approve of you? Mother, your Grandma, didn't want me endangering my own life to do the work I do. How could she want that? Daddy, your Papa, ripped down, balled up, and stomped on my Black Liberation posters. But when I was in jail, on trial, slandered, demonized, they stood by me. They supported me every moment of my life. You don't know it, but that's what your mother and I are doing for you. So stand by your own work, your own opinions. Who cares what we think or if we're critical. You don't think we want you to be just like us, do you? You're you. I'm me. You're free.

EISA
Am I living up to my name?

ANGELA
Am I? Look. Just do one thing to keep the struggle going. Just one. (*pause*) Why don't you sing to keep me moving while I get prepared for my lecture. That's who you are, Angela.

EISA
Until the philosophy
which holds one race superior
and another inferior
is finally and permanently discredited
and abandoned
everywhere is war
there's a war

CES
(*like Outkast*) Rang rang.

CES *hands* EISA *the phone.*

EISA
Hello?

MOMMY
It's your father.

ANGELA
Oh no. Shoots, where is it? My lecture.

CES
(*Tribe Called Quest*) She left her notes in El Segundo.

ANGELA
Why don't you give it then.

EISA
Your lecture?

ANGELA
There's work to do. To get it done, we all have to do it together.

> *Everyone looks at each other, then the*
> *audience.* EISA *picks up the hairbrush*
> *and we hear "122 BPM" by Jive*
> *Rhythm Trax.*

CES
Angela's Mixtape, y'all! Keep it going, feel the beat, it ain't
over yet!

EISA
Thank you for coming out tonight
it's good to see all you beautiful people in the audience
I'm feeling all the love you gave us up here, you know
who am I?
Angela Eisa Davis.
What do I do?
I make mixtapes.
On this mixtape, we change the interface, from Atari to a Wii
We feels better than sticking to the letter, catch the spirit, and
you'll be free
I love hip hop and I'm not an MC
I love my fam we put the we before me
I love hip hop and I'm not an MC
I love my fam and I guess I'm just me
who am I?
Everybody trying to make sense of this stew.
who are you?
You carry this legacy too.
I'm gonna bring my fam into this a little bit now

give em the mic, let em come straight off the dome
take it back, old school, one mo gin
Whatcha gonna do when you get out of jail?

ANGELA
I'm gonna have some fun.

EISA
What do you consider fun?

MOMMY
Fun, natural fun.

CES
Now throw your hands in the air

EISA
And wave 'em like you just don't care

CES + EISA
Somebody, anybody, everybody, scream

ANGELA
I like this, it's interesting. Thank you.

GRANDMA
can it be that it was all so simple then
back in the days

EISA
And how do we get back to the future?

ANGELA
I change

MOMMY
I've changed

CES
I change

EISA
They're why we've got change at last.

ANGELA
I'm not a tape you can play
I'm live, live, all the way live

MOMMY
I have the same intentions but
I'm not playing the same set I used to

MOMMY + ANGELA
I just slide, slide, slippity slide

ANGELA
I see more,

GRANDMA
I have seen more,

ALL
I *am* more

ANGELA
and I wonder if you can hear me comrades

GRANDMA
I wonder if you can see that I am soft
Black steel in the hour of chaos

ANGELA
I wonder brothers and sisters if you see me or just an afro if
you can see my fist unfurl and how my ears are just as open
as my mouth

MOMMY + ANGELA
and I wonder if you can hear
me comrades

MOMMY + ANGELA + CES + GRANDMA
I wonder if you can see that I am soft
Black steel in the hour of chaos

ALL
if together we can all shape this infinite moment

> EISA *pulls the tape out of the boom-box and the music goes out.*

EISA
Before we go, there are some folks we've lost we need to give some love to:

CES
Kendra Alexander
Franklin Alexander

ANGELA
Louise Patterson
Vicki Mercado

MOMMY
Herbert Aptheker
Fleeta Drumgo

GRANDMA
Jonathan Jackson
George Jackson

EISA
Aunt Elizabeth
Papa

Ruth
Annie Pearl
and Grandma.

> GRANDMA *exits through the audience.*

EISA
The porter at the airport asked me:

PORTER
How's your aunt?

EISA
And I answered: she's good.

> EISA *zips up her sweatshirt and lights bump out.*
>
> *End of Play.*

AFTERWORD | GREG TATE

The following is compiled from three emails Greg Tate (1957-2021) sent after seeing Angela's Mixtape *in 2009. His family has kindly allowed me to print an edited and condensed version. If he were alive, I'd ask for more of his dancing words. But I am grateful to have dug this up from underneath years of volcanic inbox ash: a message in a bottle that presaged this very moment.*

o

so of course my whole life flashed before me—being a movement baby myself—and of course the refuge in music and books as a result bit—not parallel stories so much as sliced from that peculiarly generational black psycho drama peculiar to those of us who had parents who wanted kids and to die for the struggle too...or just wanted to be movement rock stars too—and you being the funny, deep muhfuh you are i laughed and cried with you all the way thru —yr hair dramas, lights-kindid dramas, high school 'pick a side' dramas, and of course the ever-present mama dramas....the latter aspect which kind of hit me as central midway thru as i realized that this play— like 'back to the future'—isn't completely as billed—that it's not really about angela n you but about you n fania—that it's really fania's mixtape—a mother-daughter implosion cycle in which angela is part of the supporting cast—but a play whose emotional core is about your lifelong attempt to get fania to see hear you, feel you—and i wondered why i had never heard you talk about this piece as about that stuff...cuz fania is so front and center the easily-mocked 'villain'/wicked New Age witch in the piece and angela the transcendental surrogate mama good witch glinda...

.... at least that is until fania is given her character-revealing heroic tragic cathartic monologue moment near the end—which smacks one in the gut—because you're forced to think about the weight of being angela's sister on fania, her self-imposed need to 'live up to her name'; the burden of being the more prickly sister of a beloved mythical movement icon who is so not as fania seems, a 'movement casualty'—and to also ask yourself what it must feel like to save a man from da pigs who beats you and calls you comrade—and to raise a child who you see as the girl embodiment of said man whom you've 'disappeared' from her knowledge—which, strangely, in turn, also made me think about parts of your professional acting life, specifically 'passing strange' and 'the wire' where you, who read as early 30s boho gal, are almost typecast as this stern, judgmental middle-aged working black woman on the edge—and i thought, to what extent is the palpable fury of sweet eisa channeling lady mac-fania speaking directly to the x-ray eyes of casting agents?

'course you channeling rosie perez was pretty awesome too. fighting not the power of the state with hardcore hip hop warrior terpsichore but the power of medusa. which is to say, end of day, i experienced this as your 'elektra' play rather than an angela hagiography, an exorcism of patricidal motherly demons with appropriately Oakland-ish kumbuya moments after the sore-and-boil-popping purgings.

as always your devotion to (all your) craft(s), language, honesty and self-examination/soul-excavation rocks. and AMT also throws into relief that whole idea that all writers write the same piece over and over again—so zora, gayl jones*, the two

---

    *   Tate is referring to Zora Neale Hurston, as a character in my play *Paper Armor*, and to Gayl Jones, an inspiration for the characters and

protags of bulrusher—i now also see as triple goddess fusion figures of you, fania and angela in the eisa d. literary oeuvre... (yes think of me when it comes time to write the intro to the canonical ED collection)...your fellow cast were stellar of course, especially kim brockington.... maybe i'm overstepping de bounds of brotherly love with this unbound uncensored boundary-crossing immediacy of response—tho' to clarify i didnt mean ur writin' the same play so much as i was acknowledging that recurring trinity of women who are sometimes 3 in 1 woman—zora and gayl—and sometimes three or four— angela, bulrusher—which could also be read as very tactically toni morrisonesque—the recognition that any truthful, complex staging of just one black female persona requires at least three women being front and center in the telling..... i do gotta say it's kinda kool, kinda scary and kinda funny, if i read you correctly here, that you're kinda saying your mom took one for the home team in this telling of black matriarchs and their discontents! good to know y'all are tight like that! cuz i felt like i was getting bruised by fania's role as open wound and surgical cut—

it's brave work man. i give you major props for even being able to go there in public. i gave it up to spike and joie after crooklyn too.... think that's why i write criticism and 'science friction'... family requires love, distance and nerve.

loves ya mama, gt

---

plotline of my play *Six Minutes*. He always came with open ears to catch everything I made, music, plays, whatever, brandishing capacious insight and libraries of wildly juxtaposed knowledge, his cheerleader pompons always waving to the beat of the driest, bubbliest wit. I miss and love him. How joyous I am to have been in his ken. How lucky we all are to have experienced his writerly, musical heart.

A WORD FROM MOM | FANIA DAVIS

Angela's Mixtape is not only my daughter Eisa Davis' uber creative coming of age song that "rarely drop[s] below 100 beats per minute," as she says in the introduction, that collapses time, and that in other ways transgresses the bounds of conventional story-telling—it also fiercely proclaims her determination, in poetic notes, tones, and movements variously joyful and angry, humorous and resentful, to find her own song. It is a rite of passage opening the way for Eisa to find her true, unique, and distinctive voice. Distinct from her mother's, her aunt's, her grandmother's, and father's. Even distinct from (while also perhaps dialectically including) the cacophonous voices of revolution, black liberation, and Marxism that dominated life in her early years.

Reading and watching *Angela's Mixtape* left me in an emotional swirl of deep self-reflection. My sense is that the rite of finding herself has meant that Eisa has felt compelled to remove herself from the shadow of her mother's often overbearing tree. At the same time, it compelled me to look in the mirror and see myself as I was then in all my dogmatic revolutionary zeal and fervor. I initially told Eisa I didn't recognize myself in *Angela's Mixtape*. After some introspection, I realized how challenging it's been for me to admit how incredibly heavy and hard coming up under me must have been for a deeply sensitive, creative child like my daughter. I am sorry that I didn't have the wisdom then to know that I could be both a zealous and fervent revolutionary and a deeply loving, attentive and caring mother to my daughter. And for that, I am so sorry, my beautiful and amazing child.

To find her own song, Eisa has also needed to remove herself to some degree from the massive shadow of her aunt's colossal tree. Though these bounteous trees have also been sources of comfort and shelter, *Angela's Mixtape* boils down to a search for light—Eisa fiercely moving through shadow to find the light that will allow her to grow her own tree, unstunted, rising to its full glory.

—Fania Davis

NOTES | EISA DAVIS

As an artist, you get to serve your work's needs, whatsoever they may be. To scale heights and plumb depths you never would have before, to dispense with comfort and looking cute, to get dirty and make something lean. But in life it can be harder to abide by that tenet, to make hard choices that will ultimately nourish you and the world. To rebel, cut yourself off from what you know, run towards what you are most afraid of—to individuate from your family tree and plant yourself in the sunlight, as my mother wrote—can be quite difficult. It has been for me. In the autobiographically based pieces in this volume, I am hoping to serve the needs of both work and life. Speaking truths that I'm not expected or encouraged to reveal is not meant to hurt anyone, but rather to undo the hurt that silence can instill. My aunt, mother, and father are all outspoken, must always call out injustice when they see it, and I've inherited my own version of that, in my own realms. I know how dangerous it is and has been for black folks, and women, and black women, to speak truth that may lose us our lives and livelihood and community. The risk is real—my aunt's experience with the state being a most extreme example. But she dares to speak. Cannot do anything but that. And in so doing she helps to liberate the world. The same goes for my mother and my father. So I try to live up to my name. When I speak in my version of our forthright family style, I've certainly been shown the door or ghosted or subtly, imperceptibly dismissed. But I've also witnessed painful dynamics transform into healthier, freer ones within institutions, work settings, and relationships of all kinds, and felt aspects of my being flourish simultaneously. Compassionate, accountable, brave clarity can do real work.

And this intrepid, searingly honest, utterly wondrous reflection that my mother has written in response to *Angela's Mixtape* moved me to tears—and moved us into a new phase in our bond. When I wrote this play, I wasn't looking for her to apologize. Instead, I hoped to celebrate the distinctive, unique childhood she, Angela and the Bay Area gave me, to document that crucial sociopolitical moment in time, and to reveal how our mutual transformations have taken place. If she's apologizing, then I should apologize for just being a teenager, filled with the unconscious rage of feeling unheard and unloved. Neither of us had the ability to listen then in the way we do now—nor did we have the privilege of hindsight. So I did not expect or want an apology. But she tells me that apologizing was what she needed to do.

We keep growing together. That a relationship more formative than all others could mutually evolve? It's a rare blessing. My mother is not the "prickly" "movement casualty" Tate surmises from my child's viewpoint—but a woman who has recreated herself over and over by listening deeply to her soul and to the people she loves. She and my aunt have given me powerful models of how, as Carl Hancock Rux sang, the only revolution is our evolution.

Angela shared a sentiment similar to my mother's in a 2011 interview with *The Los Angeles Times*: "I came to recognize how difficult it must have been for [Eisa] to make her own way through a web of expectations about education, career paths and political commitments. [*Angela's Mixtape*] allowed me to more deeply appreciate the determination with which she created her own path."

That determination has not been constant. Like the characters of Eisa in *Angela's Mixtape* and Soph in *The History of Light*, I am still searching for my fit in the world, a fit which can elude me each time I think I have found it, a fit I remind myself comes into existence only when I create it, in community. When I grow together with my people.

Growing means sharing the story that is true for me, regardless of my fear of reprisals, or cultures of secrecy. As the child in *Angela's Mixtape*, I sensed a pattern of being punished when I shared my truth, and as the immature adult in *The History of Light*, I was also ashamed of what my truth was. In our daytime rehearsal after the very first preview of *Angela's Mixtape* in New York, our director Liesl asked me how I was doing. She was right to ask: I was off my game. I was not committing with full force, not performing at the level she knew I could. When she pressed me to tell her what was going on, I admitted that I wasn't sure if the play was any good. I have no idea what her internal reaction to that question was. But her response to me, in a very matter of fact tone, was, "Would any of us be working on this play if it weren't good?" Oh right. Good point Liesl. Our family of actors and designers and producers aren't just humoring me. Gotcha. "You had the courage to write this down," she said, "and now you have to have the courage to say it aloud and mean it." And I heard her, but only in my ears. That night, when I ran out yelling like Flavor Flav at the top of the show, I saw the house lights shining bright on a man sitting in one of the front rows with his pen and notepad. I recognized him as one of the main theatre critics from *The New York Times*, preparing to assess us for the paper of record. His presence switched something on inside me—and suddenly I felt Liesl's call to courage with my whole body. Fuck it, I said to myself, with full hip hop braggadocio. You, Mr. Critic, are going to get the dopest show imaginable. You wanna be up here judging me? Go right ahead. And he did. He judged us—with a favorable review. Which shouldn't have the power it does, but it was way better for us than a dis. Liesl made sure

I grew. Made sure I brought the tiger out of its cage, and rode it—for and with all of the ladies in the cast, who remain a family 14 years later. Growing together.

I've also grown immensely with my father. *The History of Light* premiered just a few months after we finished our run of *Angela's Mixtape*, with Liesl at the helm again. If *Angela's Mixtape* was my mommy play, *The History of Light* was my daddy play, exploring how my lack of relationship with him affected my romantic relationships, represented by one relationship in particular. Interplay between two interracial couples over two different eras provide the engine of the story—but unlike *Angela's Mixtape*, *The History of Light* is fiction, built for narrative effect. It borrows mercilessly from two epistolary relationships: one between me and a dear friend of mine slash would be paramour, and another between my father and his first love in college. Some of it happened, and a lot of it did not. It's all convoluted, angled toward my self-interest and effective storytelling. I made the character most like myself, Soph, look wild and pitiable, desperate, awful, occasionally heroic (maybe?). In creating Math, I ridiculed my dear friend and his wife whom I love and care for via unfair caricatures commonly created by the rejected and hurt. And Turn, inspired by my father, got similar fast and loose treatment—a characterization influenced by dramatic needs and the real woman (codename Suze) who gifted me with my father's love letters to her. That was real. So I stole from our lives for the play, but the play takes potshots that I personally do not endorse. The opinions expressed are not those of the author, but of the play. It's fiction, thank goodness, fueled by actual events and feelings, and since you don't know what is what, assume it's made up.

My father and I had many arguments about the play's content, mainly over email. Much of what he took issue with were the *fictional* aspects of character, action and dialogue relating to the character most like him. I altered some things for the second production, the text for which is printed here. But in the process of his setting the record straight about his own life—he was frustrated that I didn't know what I couldn't have known without him telling me—I learned things about him and he learned things about me that never would have come up otherwise. And in the course of those arguments, we fostered a new understanding of each other. We have bathed in our own history of light, as my father put it, finding a new mode for our interactions with one another. Rereading our email exchanges after he read and viewed the play, I realize that the past has been kneaded and worked and threshed and that we are now left with the present, which, like a child, is birthed by the past but not consigned to it. It's my responsibility to make something nourishing of my relationship with him. And as an apparently grown ass woman, if I need anything he (or my mother) can't give, I get to parent myself.

To be his emissary, I have to address a couple of crucial points on how he is depicted in both plays. Against how Turn is shaded in *The History of Light*, my father did not marry my mother because she was "the perfect black woman" as Suze asserts. His choice, he says "had to do with my search for a lover/comrade with whom I could trust my life. In this Fania has no equal—nonpareil." And regarding how he is referenced in *Angela's Mixtape*, my father has admitted to the harm that he did to my mother. He assures me he has not done anything remotely like it since. To date, my mother and father have not talked substantively about their relationship in a way that would possibly make them feel understood by the other. I have tried to make that conversation happen actively for a while. I surprised them with a reunion dinner around Thanksgiving the same year that both plays premiered. It was the first time that the three of us had had dinner together in my conscious memory. And uncannily, they were both wearing matching scarab rings. All these years apart and yet bound somehow. When I pulled a disappearing act so that they could speak one on one, which unsettled my mother, the most urgent, truest words weren't said. Maybe one day they will speak if it is what they wish. It is up to them.

So no tell-all vilification here—of course it's the opposite. I love my beautiful family, so much. Asked for their words here so they could have their say. They have made me, grown me. They have been incredibly generous in making it their business to support my work, often flying to see plays multiple times, and living through the discomfort of seeing versions of themselves onstage. My stepsister Kafí and my stepfather Larry are very much part of that family, and I want to thank them in particular. Because while my child's POV has rendered them supporting players in the tales told here, they are still very much in my life and joyfully so. I'm thankful for all they've taught me, and for the ways in which we've reimagined our relationships as well.

One other thing to mention. Formally, *The History of Light* bounces in and out of naturalism due to its scenic design and children's games set on a playground. One review of the play, which also contained a helpful note to correct the party of those who challenged the Civil Rights Act's passing from Republicans to Southern Democrats, which I have done, said the playground scenes stood out as an aspect that typified the writer's overwhelming disdain for the play. I don't wish to take this moment as an opportunity to explain myself or to respond to a writer whose review I disregard, but I do wish to contextualize my placement of the characters on the playground as the evocation of a pure place of joy for me,

the place where Soph and Math first met, a place which sym-
bolizes the youth of Turn and Suze first meeting in college. A
place where race and gender and cultural hierarchies are being
learned, tested, but have not yet fossilized into structures of
consciousness. This imaginary space of play stems from a real
ecstatic experience—my time in 6th grade that I mention in
Angela's Mixtape—and allows the characters their longstand-
ing, world-defying love. For a time. But the liberatory feeling
of the playground, and Soph's return to it in the last image of
The History of Light, is indelible for all the characters, and for
me, as a kind of home.

In one talk she included in her book of essays *The Source of
Self-Regard*, Toni Morrison postulated a space where race does
not matter yet still exists: not as a utopian, heavenly house, but
as home. I believe that my practice has always been to write
from and through that homeplace she delimits—toward inqui-
ry, connection, liberation—and that both these plays extend
from the experience of trying to understand home more deeply. This stance centers experiences that are decentered by the
dominating forces of our society—and therefore subverts that
power without raising its voice.

Down the street from where I write this, there is a beautiful
mural painting by Dr. Nettrice R. Gaskins of Greg Tate The
Infinite overlooking Betty Carter Park in Fort Greene, Brooklyn. I'm glad I get to see Tate as Buddha smiling in music when
I take a walk in the hood, that I get to thank him for his unbe-
lievable intellect and spirit.

And somehow the Isley Brothers' "Harvest For The World", a
favorite of my mother's, has been on my mind lately. Can you
hear her playing that song in the mornings, ushering in hope,
joy, and warmth with the dawn? How she created a home
where she built her dreams, letting the music sing her into

a future beginning in that moment? And so I have always wanted to do what she loved, to perform for her; make that music, that art for her; say all the things I couldn't say, feel all the things I wasn't supposed to feel. That's what I'm still doing now, growing, with her, with Angela, with my father, with you.

—Eisa Davis
October 2023
Brooklyn, New York

THE

HISTORY

OF

LIGHT

PRODUCTION HISTORY

The History of Light was commissioned by Marge Betley at Geva Theatre Center, Mark Cuddy, artistic director. It received workshops there and at New Dramatists before its premiere in July 2009 at the Contemporary American Theater Festival, Ed Herendeen, artistic director.

Cast

MATH | Jason Denuszek
SUZE | Lee Roy Rogers
TURN | David Emerson Toney
SOPH | Amelia Workman

Design + Production

Lights | Colin Bills
Costumes | Trevor Bowen
Scenic | Robert Klingelhoefer
Sound | Matt Nielson
Production Photos | Ron Blunt

The History of Light was subsequently produced at the Passage Theatre Company in Trenton, New Jersey, November 3 – 20, 2011, directed by Jade King Carroll.

CHARACTERS

SOPH (SOPHIA). Black woman, early 30s.
MATH (MATTHEW). White man, early 30s.
TURN (TURNER). Black man, late 50s.
SUZE (SUSAN). White woman, late 50s.

Actors double as:

DICK (DICK GREGORY, a black man played by SOPH)
HUNT (TATE HUNTER, a white man played by MATH)

TIME

2002. And the past.

PLACE

The city, the country, the mind.

SET

A playground with a swing set, benches, and a piano on it.
The other environments of the play emerge from or can be
added to these basic elements.

NOTE

A dash at the end of a line (—) means to stop talking suddenly when interrupted by another character or thought. The sentences are meant to be left unfinished.

Lee Roy Rogers and David Emerson Toney in *The History of Light*.

Jason Denuszck and Amelia Workman in *The History of Light*.

MOVEMENT ONE

ANDANTE CON MOTO

> SOPHIA *is finishing her set in a divey,*
> *hip club. She sings at the piano, eyes*
> *closed, accompanying herself.*

SOPH

Maybe I'll say maybe tonight
It ain't romance but it sure ain't a fight
We pull the wool right over our own eyes
Might not be love but we can compromise

When we met I wasn't feeling good
My heart lay still, in a coffin made of wood
You didn't care, you didn't want to be alone
And I wanted someone to call me on the phone

> *As the song progresses, the rueful*
> *aspect fades and she becomes pos-*
> *sessed by something.*

When will we end this sour charade
I know the costs have already been weighed
We know too much and pretend we don't know anything
What hurts more—to give up or do the same old thing

Maybe I'll say maybe tonight
I don't know if it's wrong or if it's right
There's nothing left inside to tell me why
When you ask "Do you love me?" I say "Maybe," tonight

> SOPH *returns to self-consciousness.*
> *A moment. She is gleaming with*
> *some vengeful power.*

Thank you. Thanks for coming out tonight.

> *The audience now understands they
> can applaud.* SOPH *fixes her bra
> strap and finds her drink. She starts
> to knock her drink back but sees*
> MATTHEW *coming up to her and can't
> help but laugh with shock.*

SOPH
What???? Oh my God. Oh my *God*, not you...

MATH
You didn't look at me the whole show. I felt like a sea lion.
Clapping, clapping. Don't I at least get one look?

SOPH
I forgot what you looked like.

MATH
No you haven't.

> *They stare, unsure of what to say or
> do with their bodies. Awkwardness.
> Then they begin talking with no air
> between their sentences, testing the
> waters.*

MATH
You were an earthquake.

SOPH
Like 1 point—1?

MATH
I'd say 6 point 4.

SOPH
Math. I can't believe you're really here.

MATH
Math. You're the only one who calls me that.

SOPH
I'm the only one with the right to.

MATH
That picture in the paper did not do you justice. Wait, I think I remember this dress.

SOPH
It's new. To you at least. Anything I bought in the last decade would look fresh to you.

MATH
God you look good. You must be in love.

SOPH
Didn't you hear that song I just sang?

MATH
You're an artist. How do I know what's real?

SOPH
You don't.

MATH
Well, is someone gonna beat me up for talking to you?

SOPH
I actually just dumped my big ham-fisted boyfriend for a chicken noodle who understands me.

MATH
Those chicken noodles. You have a weakness for

SOPH
Chicken?

MATH
Noodles.

SOPH
At least they stick to the wall.

MATH
You're wasting your time with another noodle.

SOPH
He's an alcoholic on Prozac. He needs someone. What about you?

MATH
Your love life is immensely more interesting.

SOPH
You've always got someone around, who is she?

MATH
There's nothing to share about her.

SOPH
Is she "like a piece of furniture that makes your house a home"? That's what you said about one of them.

MATH
That was high school. This one's different.

SOPH
"She has no attention span, but we've got a good sex life." That one?

MATH
College. I think your memory qualifies as a weapon of mass destruction.

SOPH
Maybe we should try to forget everything. I'm sorry, you were talking about your current girlfriend?

MATH
Well, this one, this woman, she's—well—I don't think I can burn her up.

SOPH
She must be terribly healthy.

MATH
She doesn't seem to have any issues.

SOPH
I'm sorry to hear that.

> MATH *studies the piano without touching it.*

MATH
This piano is interesting. The action and the clarity up top seem to suit you. I could stand it giving you a little more warmth under your voice though.

SOPH
I'm gonna go take care of some—

SOPH
I like how it sounds. Uncared for.

MATH
I haven't heard you sing since college.

SOPH
That's all I been doing since, so...

MATH

Soph, when I started getting messages from you, I just
didn't know how to return them—

SOPH

We're all busy.

MATH

I've wanted to talk to you. Really. Every day since that
night at the airport.

SOPH

I know how it is.

MATH

No, you don't. You can't imagine the *throughput* of my
days. But to wade through sixty voicemails and then get
a message from you that's nothing but music, just you
playing the piano for a minute or two—I can't thank you
enough. So this is Matthew returning your call.

SOPH

Given your penchant for speechifying, that was a short one.

MATH

Being patient with me is one of the joys of knowing me.

SOPH

I think you started giving speeches back on the playground
at Briarhill. I've been thinking about it lately and here you
are.

MATH

Our elementary school is where I learned everything I
know.

SOPH
Except for your inexplicable taste in women.

MATH
There were no women on that playground, only girls.

SOPH
(*sees someone*) They're waiting for me.

MATH
How's your mom?

SOPH
Good. Wait. Is that why you're here? Is your mom doing alright?

MATH
Retired. Still smoking. Won't go to the doctor.

SOPH
And your dad?

MATH
He's sort of reached the point where he realizes he's not going to win a Nobel Prize for physics. Seems to care about spending time with me now, clears his schedule when I visit. Weird. What about your dad?

SOPH
What about him?

MATH
Well maybe you're in contact by now.

SOPH
I didn't grow up with him so it's not like I'm missing anything.

MATH
But if he knew what *he* was missing—

SOPH
He doesn't care who I am. You think you can't return phone calls? He's a lot better at it.

    Finally they pause.

MATH
It's good to see you.

SOPH
Yeah.

MATH
I'm sorry it's been so long.

SOPH
Yeah.

    MATH *touches the piano. Then it*
    begins again.

MATH
I need to ask you something.

SOPH
No.

MATH
I wouldn't ask you unless it was important.

SOPH
Math, I've *got* to pay the band. And there are other people here besides you I need to say hello to.

MATH
My life is changing. You hit thirty and then...don't you

feel it? There's this new air lapping at me, streaming under the crack of my office door. It's like I was a bird asleep in a tree and I forgot the sun was going to rise. But then it did and my chest is puffing out and I'm scraping my feet on the branch all without even thinking about it and there's only one thing left for me to do, open up my beak and—

SOPH
Just ask me.

MATH
But I need a lot of paragraphs around it.

SOPH
Contextualize it later.

MATH
Come with me tomorrow.

SOPH
What? Where.

MATH
You'll see.

SOPH
Aren't you a bird with a job?

MATH
Since I made partner I have a bit more latitude to self-schedule.

SOPH
Well I don't. I've got a rehearsal tomorrow.

MATH
Can't you change it?

SOPH
Can't you? I really was fine before you showed up.

MATH
Did you really think we'd never speak again?

SOPH
I haven't left you a message in four years or something. I mean this whole thing is stupid.

MATH
You're not glad to see me?

SOPH
I don't want to find out.

MATH
I need you, Soph. There's nothing wrong with that, is there?

Pause. SOPH *exhales.*

SOPH
Where do you suddenly need me?

MATH
(*smiles*) It's a surprise.

SOPH
Fuck that. Tell me.

MATH
I won't unless you let me give a speech.

SOPH
Damn. Give it.

> MATH *opens his mouth and follows* SOPH. *At the same moment,* SUSAN *enters, speaking her letter as*

she passes it to SOPH. MATH *exits,*
talking soundlessly. SOPH *walks to a*
swing with the letter, listening.

SUZE
Dear Sophia,

My name is Susan Hunter and I'm an old friend of your
father's. I live in Paris with my dear husband Jean-Daniel,
and I have something here that I want to send you.

SUZE *trots over to* SOPH, *and jumps*
into a swing next to her.

I've been going through all my old boxes and files of letters
and clippings and journals, and in my Turner Samson
collection, I found a ring that your father gave me when
we were in college together. We had no money but Turner
wanted to give me something for Christmas. I think it had
belonged to his grandmother. After we parted, I always felt
that this ring should go to Turner's daughter, to a woman
of the next generation. It's taken me a while to actually find
you, especially since you carry your mother's name, but
now with Big Brother internet I have no excuse!

Here's a photo I took of him in the meantime. I think he's
just 18. Now, I understand all this may be a bit awkward,
hearing from some stranger across the Atlantic. So feel free
to ignore this letter if you wish. Just know that my only
intention is to return an heirloom to your family.

Sincerely,

Susan Hunter

SUZE *and* SOPH *jump out of their*
swings simultaneously, and SOPH
stares at the photo.

*Like Dorothy clicking her heels
three times,* SOPH *suddenly begins
jumping hopscotch with her eyes
closed, taking her back to her
childhood playground. In* SOPH'S
imagination, her father, TURNER,
*enters, looking just as he does in the
photo.*

SOPH
Turner. Turn. Turn. Why are you here?

> SOPH *is invisible to* TURN. *He avoids
> her body but never acknowledges
> her presence. He only responds
> to* SUZE *and* MATH, *who also step
> onstage into* SOPH'S *mind.*

SOPH
(*re:* SUZE *and* MATH) You too? Well I wanna play. I'm good
at games. Ace King Caller!

> *A school bell. Everyone huddles up
> with one foot forward. With each
> word,* SOPH *touches each shoe in the
> circle they've made, choosing who
> will be It.*

SOPH
My mother said to pick the very best one and you are are
are are are are are are are are are are IT!

> MATH *is It. The others all run to hid-
> ing places on the playground.* SOPH
> *tries to hide behind* TURN.

SUZE
He'll never find me I'm small and I can disappear under my angel hair

TURN
He'll never find me I'm a tree

SOPH
He'll never find me I'm a song and everyone sings me without even knowing the words

MATH
These games are so juvenile. There's no logic or skill involved. I'm not improving myself in any way by playing this.

> *He plays dead. Everyone is silent.*
> *Eventually they start to peek out of*
> *their hiding places and whisper to*
> *one another.*

SOPH
What's he doing.

SUZE
He's playing dead.

TURN
But he's It, that's not the game. He has to come and get us.

SUZE
He doesn't want to.

> *They all stare at him. In full voice,*
> *they gripe.*

SOPH
This isn't fun. We aren't running. We aren't chasing.

TURN
We aren't being chased.

> SUZE *lays down next to* MATH. *He doesn't move.*

SOPH
Your shoe is touching his pants, that means *you're* It. Chase us!

SUZE
No, he has to touch me with his *hands* to make me It.

TURN
What if *you* touch him.

SOPH
Yeah touch him then you'll be It and you can chase us!

SUZE
I don't know if it works that way.

SOPH
Touch him.

TURN
Do something. I want to play.

SOPH
But don't kiss him 'cause we're not playing Kissing Girls, we're playing tag.

SUZE
Okay.

> SUZE, *still lying next to him, puts her hand on* MATH. *He doesn't move.*

TURN
God, what's wrong with him?

> SUZE *stretches her leg over* MATT.

TURN
That's humping.

SOPH
They're not humping!

SUZE
I'm checking his pulse. (*She does.*) It's low! Look at his face!

SOPH
He's turning Slurpee! He's a blue Slurpee!

TURN
(*leans in*) He isn't breathing.

SOPH
We have to do CPR!

SUZE
That's kissing, so I can't. I'm a virgin!

SOPH
I'll do it. But I'm *still* a virgin.

> SOPH *gets close, then hesitates.*

SOPH
What if I kiss him wrong and kill him?

TURN
(*to* SUZE) I think you have to jump on his chest and wake up his heart.

SUZE
Let's just shake him.

> *They start shaking him. He is limp and they drop him, scared.*

TURN
I won't call you fugly anymore if you come back to life.

SUZE
Come back to life and you can say we made out behind the bungalow.

SOPH
You can say you beat me in the 100 yard dash if you come back to life, but no one will believe you because I'm fast like really fast fast—

> *Suddenly* MATH *sucks in a big breath and in one sweeping motion, taps all of their arms.*

MATH
You're all It. Go chase each other.

SOPH
Why did you trick us?

TURN
(*impressed*) That's stamina. How'd you learn to hold your breath for so long?

SUZE
That wasn't nice.

TURN
Or sugar.

MATH
Or spice!

The boys walk off laughing.

SOPH
Turner!

He doesn't respond. SUZE stalks off.
SOPH hopscotches out of her vision,
then stares at the letter from SUZE.

Next day. A piano hall. Lots of
piano music being played simultane-
ously, echoing. Big booming chords
from a concert grand; high pitched,
tinny melodies from a spinet, etc.
The variety is overwhelming but
each piano sounds distinguishable.

MATH looks at the piano onstage
and after a few moments, as if he
has entered a vacuum, the sounds
from the other pianos are suddenly
gone.

MATH walks around the piano.
He examines it, wipes off invisible
specks of dust. He unlocks the piano
cover with a key and opens the top.
SOPH stands with jacket and bag on,
looking away from him.

MATH sits down at the piano.

MATH
What do you think. Is this the one?

SOPH
You have to play it first.

MATH
I don't know. Outta practice.

SOPH
I could just go.

MATH
No. Just—okay. Um...

> *A moment—then he plays something thoughtful—the andante of Brahms' Intermezzo No. 2 in A Major. His playing puts* SOPH *on the brink of tears. He stops playing without looking at her, but he has felt her reaction.*

MATH
So what do you think?

SOPH
I'm not thinking.

MATH
The rain, all the humidity today, it's muddying up the bass. It's still stiff—

SOPH
I can't believe you're playing again. Sounds like you never quit.

MATH
(*looking at his hands*) I can't believe there's still music in here. But how does the piano sound? These keys are almost

crunchy—

SOPH
They'll loosen, you know that. I don't know why you
brought me here. This piano is made for you. You don't
need me to tell you to buy it.

MATH
But what does it do to you? How would you describe its
quality?

SOPH
I can't know until I play it.

MATH *looks at her.*

SOPH
And I'm not going to.

MATH
It's a $50,000 piano. A Steinway B. I can't buy this without
your expertise.

SOPH
Why do you suddenly want to pick up and play again?

MATH
I need music right now, I can't say why. (*thinks*) I work—
and I'm great at my work. I'm esteemed by my colleagues,
I've been fast tracked to partner quicker than anyone in the
history of the firm—

SOPH
But now that you've got the golden fleece you don't care.

MATH
(*taking his time to make his point*) I don't *have* to fend
off things that would inhibit my development. I could

believe in a lot of the things that shackle me. Like—there's this ethos I breathe in that says you somehow have to be bivouacked under an overhang to make good things, that some portion of you has to be cursed to sculpt greatness. But I can't regress that onto the golden mean by which I imagine my life might be governed. Music *and* business. An equal attention. So I want you to misinterpret me in the direction of my own best interest. Which is the second best skill in argument.

SOPH
What's the first?

MATH
To convince you of my position in the midst of dispersions I myself I have set up. Play.

SOPH
I don't play classical anymore.

MATH
Then start again like me.

> SOPH *sits. Then she plays Debussy's Reflets dans l'eau.*

MATH
Pretty. What is that?

SOPH
Debussy.

MATH
Of course. I like that cadence.

SOPH
This piano is beautiful. It can open up to anything, it likes

if you tell it where to go... all it needs is devotion.

> SOPH *repeats the opening chords of*
> *the Debussy, singing her own lyrics*
> *on top of it.*

SOPH
I live underwater, like a post on a pier
I groan and creak when the waves come near
I don't have a day without salt and wet
The moon it keeps rising and it never seems to set

MATH
Why do you do that?

SOPH
What. Write songs?

MATH
Write such sad songs.

SOPH
They're the only ones that come out.

MATH
You aren't just a broken heart.

SOPH
No? What am I?

MATH
You're—a comet. You pop and light people up. You can.
You could.

SOPH
It's your job to improve me?

MATH
How 'bout this one?

> MATH *scoots* SOPH *over on the*
> *bench and starts to play another*
> *Debussy piece—Bruyeres—next to*
> *her.* SOPH *stands up.*

MATH
Mm. Nice. You hear that?

SOPH
Pentatonic, yup.

MATH
Would you check the barometer? Gotta know how this
piano responds to pressure. Where are we at?

SOPH
I'm *so* not your secretary.

MATH
I'm just asking you a favor.

SOPH
When have you ever done *me* a favor?

MATH
Soph—

SOPH
Why do you think you can *pretend* with me? Pretend to be
benevolent? You're a poison. You're a chronic infection, a
terminal disease.

MATH
Impressive.

SOPH

No, you are. You can't even say you're *sorry*? You can't say "That night at the airport, oops, my bad"?

MATH

You're the one who stopped us from talking.

SOPH

You just play our fucking Brahms ten years later like you're flipping on the radio? Bullshit. Arrogant. You're oblivious.

MATH

How 'bout you leaving your musical interludes for me at work. Were they really for me? Or was that your passive aggressive version of an apology?

SOPH

Please.

MATH

Gotta be perfect or I'm despicable.

SOPH

If you cared at all you might not have abandoned me. Believe it or not, I'm still not used to it.

MATH

Well I'm not like your father. I'm actually here. I'm trying.

> SOPH *grabs his hand and squeezes the fingers.*

SOPH

Do you want it back?

MATH

Ow, my god—

SOPH
Do you want it back? I play all the time so I'm stronger than you—

MATH
Uncle.

SOPH
Uncle who?

MATH
Uncle Bach!

SOPH
Which Bach?

MATH
Johann! Goddammit. Johann Sebastian Bach! (*he expects to be let go, but isn't*) What?

SOPH
Is he black or white?

MATH
What?

SOPH
Johann Sebastian Bach, black or white?

MATH
He's black!

> *She lets go. He tackles her to the floor and they wrestle. She hits her head on the piano and makes a noise. He gets her arms underneath her and sits on her legs. He checks his fingers on the hand she grabbed.*

He's fine.

MATH
I'm so fucking pissed at you. Are you alright?

SOPH
I'm so fucking pissed at *you.*

> *He lets her go. She gets up.*

SOPH
I am not doing this again. And in your kind of place, where (*she yells*) NO ONE WILL SAVE AN INNOCENT BLACK WOMAN FROM BEING ATTACKED!

MATH
That's right.

> SOPH *gets her bag and starts to leave.* MATH *grabs her hand.*

SOPH
Stop.

> *He lays her hand on his face and then moves it down to his neck.*

SOPH
There's nothing more here. The well has run dry.

MATH
Sh.

SOPH
I'm not yours, not yours anymore. You gave me up, I gave you up. Let me go.

MATH
You dreamt about me last night, didn't you?

Pause.

SOPH

No. But I imagined you on the playground. You played dead. You were It but you wouldn't chase me.

MATH

I don't have to chase you.

SOPH

I don't want you to.

MATH

Then why won't you check the barometer?

SOPH

Because you can't tell me what to do. You're not my father.

He goes to read it.

MATH

It's not as high as I thought.

SOPH + MATH

44.

MATH

(*marveling at her perfect guess*) Explain that.

SOPH

I didn't have to read it. I just knew. You've forgotten all about pianos.

MATH

Say it again.

SOPH

What.

MATH
44.

SOPH
44.

MATH
Sing it.

SOPH
(*speaks*) 44.

> *They laugh.*

MATH
(*a discovery*) I can't believe how much I've missed you.

SOPH
You want to be friends?

MATH
Not right now. Right now I want to kiss you.

SOPH
Should I call my boyfriend and see if it's all right?

MATH
No. I'll just have sex with my girlfriend tonight instead.

> *They are quiet a minute. He plays*
> *the piano ominously, Chopin's*
> *Prelude No. 20. This makes them*
> *laugh again.*

SOPH
My father's college girlfriend wrote me. From France.

MATH
Whoa.

SOPH

I know. She found me online. Sent me a picture of him. I'd never even seen a *picture* of him. I wrote her back.

MATH

Why did she write you?

SOPH

I don't know. Maybe she's trying to say something to him. Oh well, wrong tree.

> SOPH, *shell back on, gets up to leave. She doesn't look at* MATH.

MATH

You have to come back here and visit the piano again with me soon. When it's a different pressure in here. Okay?

SOPH

Uh huh.

MATH

I'm not a poison if you don't want me to be.

SOPH

Uh huh.

> *He starts to play the prelude again. She listens a bit, then leaves.*
>
> SUZE *enters, holding a pair of sunglasses. She drops a heavy puffy envelope into* SOPH'S *lap, then places a small, letter-sized envelope in her hands.* SOPH *opens the small envelope.*

SUZE

My dear Sophia,

I was so delighted to receive your note. I had no idea that
you and your father were not in touch. Turner would speak
of you every brief time I saw him over the years, so you can
imagine this was a great shock to me. I've enclosed the last
number I had for him, in case you don't have it, and I'll do
my best to share all I know of him.

My relationship with Turner was my first important one,
and as such, had a deep impact on me. We lived through an
especially turbulent and dramatic time, so I recorded much
of it, and saved pretty much everything. I suppose I should
start with how we met.

TURN *enters.*

TURN

Hello. I see you're reading *Black Like Me.*

SUZE

(*hiding her eyes with sunglasses*) I also went to the March
on Washington. Are you political?

TURN

Not by choice.

SUZE

I'm part of a student group working in support of the Civil
Rights Bill. Perhaps you might be interested in joining us.

TURN

You're interested in civil rights?

SUZE

(*removing sunglasses and continuing letter to* SOPH) I also
happen to be very interested in family histories, Sophia,

family heritage, the past, and am very happy to be able to provide whatever information I can to help you fill in your own family history, even though it covers only a short period of years before you were born.

> SUZE *puts on her sunglasses again.*

TURN
Why don't we meet tomorrow at noon, at the tree stump in the middle of campus, and you can explain civil rights to me.

> SUZE *wears a shamrock and a green cardigan, adjusting her sunglasses nervously.*

SUZE
(*to* SOPH) We met the next day. (*to* TURN) I'm sorry I'm late. I took a St. Patrick's Day walk, lost track of the time.

TURN
I didn't mind waiting.

SUZE
(*the letter to* SOPH *again*) In our country cottage in the south of France, Sophia, I am gathering together materials to send you that have laid so long in darkness, and it's quite an extraordinary experience. Re-reading everything and remembering, the years fall away, and again I feel that fervent period of my life when I was so much in love with Turner.

> *She continues to fidget with her sunglasses.*

TURN
Why don't you just leave those sunglasses off so I can see your eyes.

SUZE

(*takes off sunglasses*) Well. Our group. The purpose is to—the group is still small but—

TURN

Susan. Happy St Patrick's Day.

They laugh.

SUZE

In opposition to the Southern senators planning a filibuster against the bill, we're organizing a weeklong student filibuster to *support* its passage. There's a lot to do and I've hardly begun. Scheduling speakers, handling press, permits, mimeographing...

TURN

I would love to help you.

SUZE

Do you think? I could use it.

TURN

Of course. Now that's settled. We can get on to other things.

SUZE

(*to* SOPH) We talked until sunset, and then took a walk along the river.

TURN

When will I see you tomorrow?

Light on TURN *fades.*

SUZE

...I was so much in love with Turner...but fortunately for me, after this re-reading of all I've sent you, I did not remain in that time warp and was able to go back to my own world with my dear Jean-Daniel, with whom I have also known tremendous love and passion.

So what is in this packet. Turner's letters to me, beginning summer 1964, ending in 1985 (including five that are xeroxed as I couldn't bear to part with the originals), my journal excerpts 1964 to '67, a whole bunch of photos, newspaper clippings, a short story, and part of an unpublished novel I wrote about us. And—the ring of course!

> SUZE *hands the ring to* SOPH, *who tries it on. It's a simple gold band. It fits perfectly.*

SUZE

I'm sure all of this is much more than you bargained for! I hope you don't feel too overwhelmed, and that this is helpful and not harmful in any way.

Warmest regards,

Susan Hunter

> SOPH *looks at the huge packet, pulling papers out and examining them. She shakes her head to clear it, and then, closing her eyes, jumps hopscotch onto the playground.*

> *In* SOPH's *imagination, there is a school bell.* MATH *runs on, and all the characters move toward each other.*

TURN

(*shaking* MATH's *hand formally*) Shall we play a game of Capture the Flag?

MATH
The weather is prime. I don't see why not.

SUZE
(*to* TURN) You're on my team.

MATH
Not fair. Who said you could call teams? We have to rock paper scissors it.

SOPH
Why don't we play Red Rover instead? Then Turn will have to talk to me.

SUZE
(*giggling*) We have to hold hands for Red Rover. (*sobering as she sizes up* SOPH) She could be fast.

MATH
She could be.

SOPH
I am not fast!

MATH
You said you were.

SOPH
I meant running.

SUZE
Fast is a homonym.

TURN
(*winking at* MATH, *to* SUZE) You mean honomym.

SUZE
Okay, honomym. Sounds the same but means two things.

Fast as in fast, and fast as in you let people touch you.

SOPH
We don't have enough people for Capture the Flag. Red
Rover!

SUZE
We don't have enough for Red Rover either.

MATH
At least Capture the Flag involves strategy. Excuse me.
Stragedy.

TURN
Which is why I suggested it.

SOPH
Fine. Turner? (*no response*) Alright. Math, you're on my
team.

> SOPH *instinctively takes* MATH's *hand*
> *and then drops it, self-conscious.*

TURN
(*to* SUZE) You're on mine.

> SUZE *giggles and draws a line to*
> *divide the playground.*

SUZE
This is our territory and that's yours. (*to* MATH) You. Don't
play dead again. When you've decided on stragedy and
hidden your flag, whistle.

> *The teams break away from each*
> *other. During the beginning of the*
> *dialogue below,* SOPH *is distract-*
> *ed and keeps looking for* TURN. *A*

Mozart andante plays intermittently.

MATH
So you're in Mrs. Temperley's class.

SOPH
Yeah, Room 4. You're in LeClerc's, right?

MATH
Mm hm, the bungalow. They couldn't fit our brains in the main building, so they had to build a temporary structure.

SOPH
Our class is smarter than yours.

MATH
Is it?

SOPH
Grades, testing, social skills, creative talent, mean IQ—we're just best overall.

MATH
Really. You know, sometimes I do feel like I'm carrying the rest of the class on my back. So I guess it was just *my* brain that needed the extra space.

SOPH
You're not smarter than me.

MATH
Do you play chess?

SOPH
Do you double dutch?

MATH
I'm studying French.

SOPH
Spanish.

MATH
How many bones are in the human body?

SOPH
206. What's the summation of i=3 up to 4 of quantity 2 times x?

MATH
That's a formula, not a real number. Is a whale a mammal?

SOPH
Is my cat?

SUZE
Would you all hurry up and hide your flags? Gosh.

MATH
You're pretty.

SOPH
You will be.

MATH
My birthday is tomorrow.

SOPH
Mine is the day after.

MATH
I play piano.

SOPH
So do I!

MATH
What pieces?

SOPH
Different things. I'm playing a piece by Kabalevsky now.

MATH
I'm working on some Beethoven.

MATH
Sonatas.

SOPH
Sonatas?

SOPH
Have you ever heard of Dvorak? He wrote these four-handed pieces you have to play with someone else.

SUZE
Flags! Whistle!

MATH
We should play one together. For our birthdays.

> *Pause.*

SOPH
Okay.

> *Pause.*

MATH
Are you fast?

SOPH
What do you mean?

> MATH *takes off his shirt and grabs her hand.*

SOPH
What?

> MATH *drags her to a corner where*

he hides the shirt.

MATH
If you're fast, then run.

> MATH *whistles, still holding* SOPH'S
> *hand.* SUZE *whistles. Then they all
> start running, screaming, chasing
> each other over the line, looking for
> the flags.*

MATH
Stay with me, Soph.

SOPH
They've broken apart. We should each guard one.

MATH
No, stay with me, they won't expect it.

SOPH
I see their flag!

MATH
Where?

SOPH
Behind the water fountains. But if we put both of them in
prison then we'll win without even having to capture it.

MATH
That's good. Good strategy.

SOPH
Stragedy.

> *They run.*

SUZE
Are you upset that I sent your daughter all your letters to me?

TURN
I don't have a daughter. What letters?

SUZE
Your beautiful love letters, the ten page ones you wrote on onion skin paper those late summer nights when we were apart.

TURN
I've never written a love letter before. But I can do my times tables up to 12 by 12.

SUZE
You're in love with me still, aren't you?

TURN
You're not even in my homeroom.

SUZE
Turner, look at me.

TURN
If I look at you I won't win this game.

SUZE
(*she pushes him playfully*) All you had to do was look at me to fall in love.

TURN
Really? That's all?

> SUZE *accidentally steps over the line*
> *into* SOPH *and* MATH'S *territory.*

SUZE
That's all. See?

MATH *tags* SUZE.

MATH
Off to prison you go, ladybug.

SOPH
Aaaaaaah-ha, aaaaaaah-ha. See? Will he free you or go for the flag?

TURN
Don't lose hope, uh—what's your name?

SUZE
You know my name. You said it over and over like a mantra. Susan.

TURN
Susan.

MATH
Well Susan, he's cruisin' for a bruisin' so don't get those hopes up too high.

TURN
You can't mean me.

MATH
I don't see any other he.

SOPH
You're going to prison, make no bones about it.

> MATH *and* TURN *engage in a serious*
> *dodgefest as* MATH *tries to tag him*
> *into prison and* TURN *tries to tag*

SUZE *free.* SOPH *blocks* TURN *from tagging* SUZE.

SUZE
To your right.

SOPH
(*to* TURN) You can't avoid me. I'm not going to disappear.

SUZE
She's right. I don't know her well but she doesn't seem so terrible you shouldn't talk to her.

TURN
Who are you talking about?

SUZE
Your daughter.

SOPH
I'm right here. Say something to me.

SUZE
Turner, talk to her. I don't mind being in prison on a play-ground; it's kind of lovely here actually.

SOPH
If you don't say anything, *you're* going to prison.

SUZE
(*to* TURN) Look out!!!

MATH *almost tags* TURN *but misses.* TURN *leans toward* SUZE *to tag her but* SOPH *blocks him.*

SUZE
Oh snart. He almost touched me.

SOPH
Whose team are you on, anyway?

SUZE
(*points at* TURN) I want us to win, but I was hoping he'd
tackle this father thing along the way.

MATH
Oh watch it Soph, he's close—

> TURN *reaches for* SUZE *and tags her*
> *free. They run for their flag, but*
> SOPH *is ahead of them. She's fast.*
> MATH *follows. As they near the*
> *flag's hiding place,* SOPH *grabs it and*
> *zips for her and* MATH'S *territory.*
> *Everyone follows her, breathless.*
> *She crosses the line and they all fall*
> *on top of each other.* SOPH *raises the*
> *flag in the air.*

SOPH
(*out of breath*) I got it. We won.

MATH
We won.

> *A school bell clangs, and they get*
> *up from the strange domino tangle*
> *their bodies have made.* SOPH *shows*
> TURN *the flag, but he doesn't see her,*
> *shaking hands with* MATH.

TURN
We'll continue next recess?

MATH

My pleasure. (*to* SOPH) Birthday Dvořák? We can use the piano in the cafetorium.

SOPH

Sure, but the high C sticks. Good luck fitting your brain into the bungalow.

> MATH *and* TURN *exit. Another school bell as* SOPH *watches them go. Then she turns to* SUZE. *They draw with chalk on the ground.*

SOPH

Why did you write me? What do you want?

SUZE

I want to—give you something. It started with the ring—

SOPH

But his letters, your journal, the article, the heavy novel—you want something else.

SUZE

After 9/11 I had to—reconnect... I was clearing out my old files. I miss home.

SOPH

Mm hm.

SUZE

I don't have any children.

SOPH

Neither does my father.

SUZE

When you told me you didn't know him I had to do something. Have you read any of his letters to me yet?

SOPH
I'll read them when I'm ready.

SUZE
Your father is brilliant. Where do you think you got it from?
He loves music too. He used to sing me songs in bed—

SOPH
I have to go.

She walks away.

SUZE
Why do you think you're so unhappy? You don't know
who you are.

> SOPH *lies on the piano bench,*
> *asleep. After a while,* MATH *walks*
> *in. He looks at her with great*
> *tenderness, ties her shoelace or*
> *buttons something on her that's*
> *come undone. She remains still. He*
> *notices the wedding band on her fin-*
> *ger and picks up her hand. He plays*
> *Brahms' Lullaby loudly. She stirs.*

MATH
Did you get evicted? You've practically moved in here.

SOPH
That's not a joke.

MATH
You need money for rent?

SOPH
Yes, but not yours.

MATH
You're welcome.

SOPH
Don't ask me again or I'll take your money and that would
be terrible for my dignity.

MATH
You don't have to live hand to mouth.

SOPH
(*a reverie*) That's what you were doing when we met. It was
fine then.

MATH
When we were ten! You're obsessed with Briarhill. And me.

SOPH
You? With your massive hair? Oh no. What a helmet head
you had. Big box of hair, Kid 'N Play, Max Headroom hair
standing straight up trying to break Olympic records and
shit.

MATH
My hair *was* kind of tall then.

SOPH
It was high like Cheech and Chong. Why aren't you at
work?

MATH
Had a couple hours between clients so I thought I'd come
and see what the piano had to say today.

SOPH

Humidity's thick, so be hard to judge it. I came here to practice because my piano at home is in bad shape. Needs tuning, some hammers replaced—and I guess I played myself to sleep. Let me get outta here. You should play by yourself.

MATH

Stay with me, Soph.

SOPH

(*registering the echo from her dream*) If you're gonna get it, you have to be alone with it. It's a big commitment.

MATH

That's why I need you. To help me decide if I want to make it.

SOPH

Do you remember Capture the Flag and—

MATH

No! The first time we played?

SOPH

Yes. I can see it all.

MATH

Dreaming again, huh? Can you have dreams about what actually happened? I've never done that. Is that neurologically possible?

SOPH

It's not dreaming. It's like—visions I hop into. Some of it happened and some never did, all interspersed.

MATH

And what did I say?

SOPH
(*flaring*) That's *all* you care about?

MATH
Easy. We're not going to wrestle like ten year-olds again
and split a seam in this suit.

SOPH
Why don't you bring me back to the office with you? That's
who you are now. I should know what that is.

MATH
You don't want to see me there. I have a different pace; it's
more transactional. When I talk, I don't trellis like when I
talk to you. There, I cut to the chase, hit winners, passing
shots, swing for the lines a lot, I won't keep volleys going.
I'm using tennis analogies here.

SOPH
Thanks for clarifying.

MATH
There I never pontificate, never seem open or insightful,
I just capture opportunity. My body language is like this.
(*He leans forward.*) I'm a vector flying into you. I'm not
sitting back. My sentences are short. No adverbs, no allit-
eration, no polish, I just hew, carve. And I'm out the door
before people can even ask, "Who was that?"

SOPH
Do you enjoy being a vector?

MATH
I meet and work with as many smart people as stupid. I get
to mentor and recruit and train new team members. I get to
use my powers.

SOPH

And you'll play this as a hobby? It's too good for that. You're too good for that.

MATH

You're different. You write music. I don't. I create when I talk. That's my job. Talking.

SOPH

And are you fulfilled by talking?

MATH

I've done some pro bono work I'm proud of.

SOPH

That's not enough. Not for you.

MATH

There's nothing wrong with not being an artist. There are other things that need to get done.

SOPH

I can't argue with that.

MATH

You don't mind being on unemployment. I do.

SOPH

I mind not having a purpose. What's yours?

MATH

I'm a leader. I just don't always know where I'm leading people to.

He plays Liszt's Consolation No. 1 under the next exchange.

SOPH

I thought of another one. Maria Callas. She's black.

MATH

Uh huh, I can see that. Callas and Pavarotti. But Renee Fleming, white.

SOPH

Peter Jennings, black.

MATH

Dan Rather, Tom Brokaw, white.

SOPH

Paul Newman, black. And Jewish.

MATH

Tom Cruise, white. Uh huh. What about Madonna?

SOPH

She exploits blackness so that's tricky. It's about whether you naturally embody a who-gives-a-fuck grace. Cate Blanchett—she's at least half black. Anthony Hopkins, Clive Owen—black people.

MATH

Condi Rice?

SOPH

Okay. There's a conflation of terms here, of course: there's the blackness that you stand in and then there's the blackness you are born in. The first you choose because it's what you are, in the second what you are is chosen for you.

MATH

Yeah, yeah, which is she. Black, black, or white?

SOPH
All of the above.

MATH
Game ain't so fun anymore, is it?

SOPH
Nothing's ever fun when you say her name.

> *He plays more Liszt; they talk.*

SOPH
This is civil. We're actually functioning like two mature adults.

MATH
Whodathunk. Skirmish free.

SOPH
I still wonder why the dramatic return from the dead. The piano I get, but why me, now?

MATH
(*stops playing*) You don't know I still love you?

> *Pause.*

SOPH
Don't say that.

MATH
There's no one like you in my life.

SOPH
And you pushed me out of it.

MATH
And I don't know why.

SOPH
If you want me back in, you better find out.

MATH
What's that ring on your finger?

SOPH
(*laughs*) Is that what this is about? You get a hot flash? You like it when I wear rings.

MATH
Well I've never seen that one before.

SOPH
You don't want me married, huh? Engaged, even?

MATH
This the noodle, he did this?

SOPH
No, your girlfriend gave it to me. You think I'm that insane? It belonged to my great grandmother. Father's side. I didn't elope, reel it back.

MATH
The woman in France sent it to you?

SOPH
Who else. She told me her father didn't want her seeing my father because he was black. Can you imagine?

MATH
When are we talking?

SOPH
1964, round there.

MATH
I can imagine some fearful minds.

SOPH
(*pause*) Play something for me.

MATH
What.

SOPH
Chopin. The Ballade in F, with that pretty part in three at the beginning.

> MATH *doesn't remember.* SOPH *starts playing it to goose his memory, humming the melody as she plays.* MATH *remembers the song and immediately opines.*

MATH
You always accent the upbeat. So weird. It's too bouncy that way. It has to feel gummy, like this...

> *He plays, placing equal accents on the up- and downbeat.* SUZE *is swinging.*

SUZE
I'm in love! I'm in LOVE!!!!

TURN
Whenever I am away from you, your prettiness increases. And when I see you again, your face is a new field of study.

> SUZE *jumps out of the swing from the top of its arc.* HUNTER, SUZE'S *father, enters, furious.*

HUNT
Are you dating him?

SUZE
Who? Turner Samson?

HUNT
Who else would I mean?

SUZE
Dad. I just met him three weeks ago.

HUNT
You're avoiding the question, Susan. Are you dating him or not?

SUZE
We've been out a few times.

HUNT
Is this your version of rebellion? You went to the March on Washington and now you want to march your cause into our friends' homes? Are you doing this to embarrass me?

SUZE
Are your friends so provincial they're reporting on a non-event?

HUNT
You know what you did.

SUZE
I didn't do anything wrong.

HUNT
I'm a Democrat, Susan. But you're jeopardizing my work in the House to get the Civil Rights Bill passed. You want to help him, be his *friend*. Not this.

SUZE
And when I tell him we can't see each other anymore, what reason should I give?

HUNT
You're ruining your life.

SUZE
What?

HUNT
Are you going to marry him? You'll be rejected by everyone. Your children will have no place—

SUZE
It's only been three weeks!

HUNT
You aren't listening to me.

SUZE
It's your fault. You raised me to forget color, and now you want me to suddenly remember it?

HUNT
You're a girl. You don't *know*.

SUZE
I know it's wrong to do what you're asking. It's you who doesn't know. You don't know *him*.

> HUNT *walks away from her. A door slams.*

SUZE
My father is a Congressman and—

TURN
WHAT???

SUZE
Yes, he's a Congressman so I think we might get some good press for our filibuster.

> *A banner: "Student Filibuster for Change. Civil Rights Now!" A photo flash.*

SUZE
(*her speech as she begins the filibuster*) As the Senate enters its 41st day of filibuster against the Civil Rights Bill, we students from campuses around the metropolitan area today begin a weeklong filibuster in *support* of the Civil Rights bill, to share with the world at large our firm belief that the vision outlined by this legislation is not only a dream but should become the reality of every man, woman and child in this country.

TURN
Good afternoon ladies, gentlemen, fellow students, passers-by, apathetics, hecklers, integrationists, white supremacists. You are all welcome here to our filibuster for change. Filibusters are usually intended to maintain the status quo, but what we offer today and this week is an urgent message: stagnation on this issue is not only regressive but deadly. We won't be reading from the yellow pages or the Bible or Cicero or Catullus, no. You will not hear stories of a people to be pitied. We have no interest in white sympathy.

> *An offstage student lobs an egg at* TURN's *head and laughs.* TURN *continues to speak, the yolk and white running down his face.*

TURN

But we do request your respect. If we are men, we deserve comparable schooling. If we are men, we deserve employment and compensation commensurate with our skills. If we are men, we should enter the same door, sit at the same counter, drink at the same fountain, walk with the same pride as the men who by calling us inhuman create this quality in themselves. If I am a man—and who here says I am not?—then we shall make a country that may rightfully call itself the *United* States of America, untouched by the strife of injustice, and bound by the joys of its freedoms.

> SUZE *helps to wipe the egg from his face.*

SUZE
Join our cause.

TURN
Fulfill the covenant of this great nation.

SUZE
Pass the bill.

TURN
Live without prejudice.

SUZE
Rapist

TURN
Nigger lover

SUZE
I see nothing but you

TURN
I see nothing but you.

> *They kiss and fall to the ground,*
> *covering themselves with the ban-*
> *ner that has now become a sheet.*
> *They've just made love.* TURN *pulls*
> *a pen from his sport jacket, places it*
> *in his mouth, inhales, and pretends*
> *to blow out smoke. They laugh.*
> TURN *begins singing along with Glo-*
> *ria Lynne's "Don't Take Your Love*
> *From Me".*

TURN
Would you take the wings from birds
So that they can't fly
Would you take the ocean's roar
And leave just a sigh
All this your heart won't let you do
This is what I beg of you
Don't take your love from me

> SUZE *lights a sparkler on a cake with*
> *fresh strawberries.*

TURN
What's all this for? Party for your roommate?

SUZE
Actually, it's Malcolm X's birthday. And Ho Chi Minh's.
And...

TURN
Is it yours? Did I forget your birthday?

SUZE

That's a good one. Do you really not remember? (*she pauses*) You don't. It's yours.

TURN

Goddamn I am some kind of fool. I am some kind of fool.

SUZE

No, don't say that.

TURN

I've never. Never celebrated my. Never been given a birthday party before. Down South we never had any—

> *He puts his hand on her face.*

TURN

Thank you. You are beautiful. You are a flower.

> *She pops a strawberry in his mouth.* SOPH *enters and sits by a fountain or a confusing public sculpture in the lobby of* MATH'S *office, sipping a chai, waiting.*

SUZE

(*sees* SOPH *waiting soberly*) Do you wanna play with us?

SOPH

No, I'm—

> SUZE *has already hopped off with* TURN.

SOPH

Have fun.

> *A taxi honks.* MATH *finally enters, annoyed.*

MATH
You threw off my whole afternoon coming here.

SOPH
(*careful*) I wanted to see you in your office. I didn't know—

MATH
No, I wanted to get out, I just—big presentation tomorrow, so I'm scheduled to the second. Are you drinking that amazing chai from the stand outside? I want some. Some kick.

> MATH *leads her out of the lobby and
> onto the street. They head toward
> the line at the chai stand.*

SOPH
What do you do in there?

MATH
Work.

SOPH
You're hiding something. Is that where you keep your old nerd self in an oxygen tent?

MATH
I was never a nerd.

SOPH
Come on, chess? Church? Math? Where do you think your nickname came from? But then junior year of high school you finally got a haircut. A tan. Contacts. A girlfriend.

MATH
(*to chaiwalla*) May I have a chai please? Large?

SOPH
With *big* hoohoos. She would drop you off at the practice

room and god the public display of affection was felonious. She even choreographed a solo to a Police song for the dance recital and dedicated it to you in the program.

MATH
I think I spent more time practicing with you than I spent with her. Why didn't you have a boyfriend then?

SOPH
I did. There were a couple of noodles, for a couple months.

> TURN *leaves the stand with his chai, and recognizes* SOPH *who is standing several feet away from* MATH. *He stops, but she doesn't recognize him, smiling at him as she'd smile at a stranger. He pauses and walks on.* MATH *has noticed him looking and walks closer to* SOPH.

MATH
We're a striking couple. People take note.

SOPH
Then why are we always with other people?

MATH
I'm just trying to tell you you're *fine*, that's all.

SOPH
I have to go to an audition in a few minutes.

MATH
(*pissy*) Okay, I rearranged and came down because I thought we were going to play the piano. (*gets his chai, and pays*) Thanks.

SOPH
That's why I came to pick you up here. I couldn't move my
audition time.

MATH
So—we can't go?

SOPH
Not today.

MATH
(*groans*) As long as this audition's not for a cruise ship.

SOPH
You are so clingy these days, you're beginning to worry me.

MATH
Tell me what it's for.

SOPH
To be an exhibit in an interactive black culture museum. I
have to sing and play Dick Gregory. Please, no comments.
I'm fucking broke.

MATH
Who's Dick Gregory?

SOPH
Really? Funniest healthiest black man on the planet? Serious
political activist. And still going.

MATH
You know me. Hip to be square.

SOPH
When are you going to decide on this piano anyway?
You're waffling.

MATH

Look I'm buying an apartment so forgive me if I'm being fiscally conservative.

SOPH

You're buying an apartment? Well let me know when I can move in! An apartment. When were you going to tell me? That's really—

MATH

Yeah. Hey, do your audition for me.

SOPH

Oh no. I can quote some letters my father wrote his girlfriend though.

MATH

You can quote them?

SOPH

They're out of control. He's writing from the 19th century or something—"when the herald of my passion has gained entrance to the warm moist hall of your woman's desire"—

MATH

Oh that's good, what else—

SOPH

Um—"there has been no finality in my love for another woman that could maintain a quarantine on my feelings from you, Susan."

MATH

Ooh, he's got it.

SOPH

"I am eager to get inside history and in some way counteract the forces that cause the history of men to aberrate from the history of light."

MATH
Damn. I'd memorize that shit too. I don't think aberrate is a word though.

SOPH
Give it to him. For eighteen that's a pretty logical invention. His eloquence is comforting. It's like I'm meeting a paper you.

MATH
What's his name again?

SOPH
Turner Samson.

MATH
Why don't you carry his last name?

SOPH
One day I just started going by my mom's maiden name, like she did, turning in my school assignments with it. I didn't want to be different from her, from my family.

MATH
I wonder what he does now. He sounds like a born writer. You still won't call him?

SOPH
Nope.

MATH
But with your photographic memory I bet you know his number by heart.

SOPH
919 356 0121.

MATH
Damn.

SOPH
And I'll never use it! I have to go.

MATH
I think about you a lot. You're on my mind.

SOPH
Thanks?

MATH
I want good things for you.

> SOPH *pecks him goodbye on the cheek and walks off.*
>
> *An impulse.* MATH *dials a number on his phone.* TURN *picks up, just a block away.*

TURN
Turner Samson.

MATH
(*thrown for a moment*) Turner Samson, please.

TURN
This is he.

> MATH *has no idea what he wants to say.*

MATH
Hello, Mr. Samson, this is Matthew Brendel. I'm calling

because I was recommended to you—your work was recommended to me by a colleague and—I think you might be
a good candidate for our firm.

> TURN *hangs up.* MATH *calls back,*
> *gets* TURN'S *voicemail. "This is*
> *Turner Samson. If you're not seri-*
> *ous, hang up. Otherwise—" beep.*

MATH
(*leaving a message*) Mr. Samson, this isn't a sales call.

> TURN *is calling him on the other*
> *line.* MATH *clicks over.*

TURN
I doubt I was recommended to you by anyone who thinks
I'd be a good candidate for your firm. I'm not a very good
employee.

MATH
That's exactly the sort of spirit we encourage here at our
company. Independent, renegade thinking.

TURN
What exactly does your firm do? Never mind, I'll look it up
myself.

> TURN *does a search for* MATH'S
> *name on his phone with his stylus.*
> *It's 2002. It takes a minute.*

TURN
I see. Oh. I see. You are all up in the Kool-Aid and can't
even comprehend the flavor, Matthew Brendel.

MATH

I assure you that I am calling with the purest of—

TURN

You're corporate.

MATH

Something wrong with that?

TURN

There is nothing more in need of blame than the capitalist attempt to convert every sacred human activity including but not limited to thought, childrearing, illness, grief, birth, death, and sex into a profit bearing enterprise. Your corporations are invented precisely in order to afford the individuals who comprise it a legal abdication of all responsibility. Which is exactly what you are doing now.

MATH

I'm not abdicating responsi—you can't escape corporations—

TURN

(*beginning to walk*) Thought you could make a lot of money without oppressing somebody? Your privilege is, by its very existence, making someone else poor.

MATH

(*finding his feet in this unexpected debate*) I don't buy that. People create new resources. That's the only way economies grow. But if you were right, you'd be just as guilty as you say I am because there are millions poorer than you.

TURN

I don't exploit anyone. You, on the contrary, make us all poor by design.

They recognize each other from the chai stand as they walk, then realize they're talking to each other on the phone. They both hang up and stand face to face.

MATH
Hi.

TURN
You afraid to keep talking to me now that you know what I look like?

MATH
Do you launch into polemics with everyone you meet?

TURN
I never miss an opportunity to educate. You are neither the way, the truth, nor the life.

MATH
It's nice to meet you too.

TURN
There's nothing nice about your system.

MATH
So what do you want to replace it with? It's 2002. Even Marx would admit that socialism isn't the answer.

TURN
We already have a mixed economy. People pay taxes, redistribute the income—

MATH
Look, it's really basic. You're self-interested and want something different and revolutionary that privileges *you*,

and I'm self-interested, sticking with a status quo I know privileges *me*. As long as you and I both have self-interest, you have no socialism. You have hungry mouths and bloodshot eyes. If you really want socialism, start a crusade to make everyone a Buddhist. You'll hit a snag in Texas, believe you me.

TURN
I like you.

MATH
I like you too. It's like we're—

TURN
Brothers from another mother?

MATH
I like that phrase. Did you coin it yourself?

TURN
Sure. Brother.

MATH
I see. Um—where were we?

TURN
We were trying to capture each other's flag.

MATH
(*a breath, then*) We're building consensus here.

TURN
Oh, you don't seem to understand. I like you but that doesn't mean I haven't dedicated my life to overthrowing you.

MATH
How 'bout we work on a solution we both can live with?

TURN

That's the project you've failed at since the first Africans were brought to slave and die on this stolen land 400 years ago. We're not going for it again.

MATH

I am your ally.

TURN

Hell no, be yourself. Don't distort your actions out of guilt. You're top dog. Admit it, enjoy it, and topple.

MATH

Don't you see? I'm having this conversation with you because we are already connected. You can't get rid of me or dismiss me. I am not "over" just as you are not "extinct." Stop looking at my face and just listen.

TURN

What?

MATH

You won't listen because of how I look. I won't call it reverse racism.

TURN

Because it isn't. Racism means I could leverage power, assets, imagery, and ideology over you like you do over me. But I can't do any of that. So I'm incapable of racism. Now, prejudice? Bias? That's a different story and I'd be entitled to sample them if I were not of the opinion, retrofitted by fact, that capitalist economics invented race. So my problem with you ain't your face. My problem is the blood on the green in your wallet.

MATH *is silent.*

TURN

You playing dead? You forfeit?

MATH

You said that childrearing was sacred. When did that occur
to you?

TURN

That's a given. That's *a priori*, a stipulation.

MATH

Is it? Or did you incorporate yourself to abandon responsibility? (*pause*) I know your daughter, Sophia Kenner. She
wasn't just standing next to me, I actually know her. Why
don't you?

> MATH *walks back into his office*
> *lobby.* TURN *stands, frozen.*
>
> SOPH *at her audition.*

SOPH

Well I can just—do you wanna hear—I'll sing the chorus?
Okay.

> *She begins to sing.* SUZE *enters,*
> *humming this same chorus to* TURN.

SOPH

(*sings "Don't Take Your Love From Me"*)
All this your heart won't let you do
This is what I beg of you
Don't take your love from me

> SOPH *takes the ring off of her finger*
> *and puts it into* TURN'S *hand, trying*
> *to capture his attention. He doesn't*

> *notice her. Then "Legs" by Daron-*
> *do plays.*

TURN

(*to* SUZE) There's a Christmas party tonight. Will you be my Juliet?

SUZE

Ugh, that sounds terrible.

TURN

Whatever you do, don't run off with Stokely Carmichael.

SUZE

He's gonna be there?

TURN

We'll see if we can get a word in edgewise.

> *The party.* DICK GREGORY *is there,*
> *holding a drink and an unlit ciga-*
> *rette in his hand.*

DICK

Have you ever stopped to think, if all the Negroes left the South, buses would ride like this? (*He tilts his forearm so the elbow and wrist are on a diagonal, elbow up.*) I know a Southerner owned an amusement park—almost went out of his mind over where to put us on a merry go round.

TURN

Oh who cares about Stokely, Dick Gregory is here.

SUZE

Well, peaches! We actually can go to a party and laugh instead of argue.

DICK

People keep talking about the white race and black race
and it really doesn't make sense. Met a fella last week two
shades darker than me—and his name was Ginsberg. Sat
down at a lunch counter and didn't get served—till he
asked for blintzes.

Isn't this the most fascinating country in the world? Where
else would I have to ride on the back of the bus, have a
choice of going to the worst schools, eating in the worst
restaurants, living in the worst neighborhoods—and aver-
age $5000 a week just talking about it?

DICK *sees* SUZE *and* TURN.

Oh now who are these two? Salt and pepper, vanilla with
fudge. Keep it in the kitchen and run from the judge. It ain't
gonna work out people!

TURN

Is that blackface you're wearing? Because you sound so
much like the Ku Klux Klan.

DICK

Oh I wish. Be nicer than turning down all their offers to
get lynched. "Hey Dick! We love your material. Why don't
you come over for LYNCH?" (*to* SUZE, *with his cigarette*)
Sweetheart, I'm just trying to cut the crap for you. We live
in America the Hypocritical. If somebody's gonna hire a
Negro to babysit so they can go to a Klan meeting, I'm a
say something. And if you think you can survive the people
who will try to kill you each day for being "in love,"
(*points to* TURN) you're Daffy and (*points to* SUZE) you're
Duck.

SUZE

We're trying to cut the crap too. The Civil Rights Bill has
passed. So it's hypocritical of *you* to think integration won't
end up in romance.

DICK

Romance. That's white for bedroom.

TURN

You think our being together is wrong?

DICK

No, I just think it's stupid. You're young, you're dreamers,
but jump out that pot before it starts boiling, now. (*turns
away from them to other party guests*) Yeah, they wanted
me to volunteer for the space program, but I turned them
down. Wouldn't it be wild if I landed on Mars and a cat
walked up to me with twenty-seven heads, fifty-nine jaws,
nineteen lips, forty-seven legs and said "I don't want you
marrying my daughter neither!"

TURN

Hell baby. Forget about him. Let him live in his world and
we'll live in ours.

TURN *gives* SUZE *the ring.*

TURN

Will you take this present from me? Something to bind us,
saying we will never tarnish?

SUZE
Turner.

SUZE *puts it on.*

DICK

(*resigned*) I hope you kids make it, I really do.

> DICK *becomes* SOPH *again.*

SOPH

(*to the people in the audition room*) Yeah. You know my father met Dick Gregory at a party once I just found out. So I um—oh do you want me to read the next scene? Oh okay. Okay. Thanks. Have a great day.

> SOPH *is at the piano and calls* MATH *on the phone.* MATH *is reading documents, trying to meet a deadline.*

MATH

(*picking up the phone*) Matthew Brendel.

SOPH

Hey it's me.

MATH

Can't talk. Deadline.

SOPH

Don't talk, just listen.

MATH

Can't listen either.

SOPH

Just put me on speaker and I'll accompany you.

MATH

Soph—

SOPH

I wrote you a song. It's short.

She begins to play it. No words,
just a beautiful, simple melody over
arpeggios. MATH *tries to work, but*
the music distracts him. He's moved.

SOPH
That's the beginning.

MATH
Play it again.

SOPH *plays it. Pause.*

MATH
You are magic. You are the closest thing to divine I've ever known in human form.

SOPH
I broke up with my noodle.

MATH
Play it again.

SOPH *plays it, and hangs up gently.*
SOPH *writes to* SUZE.

SOPH
Dear Susan,

There's someone in my life I want to tell you about. Maybe you can tell me if he's worth everything I want to give him. You might understand my feelings for him best if I explain how we are tied together, legato, contrapuntally.

MATH
Competition is fun, but there should never be a competition in music.

SOPH
(*to* SUZE) He won the competition! I lost.

MATH
We won the ensemble division playing four hand Schumann
together.

SOPH
But in the solo piano category they picked you. Because you
played better. (*to* SUZE) I hate losing, so I quit. And he said

MATH
The one thing you have that so few do? You listen. You see.
Not what's said or shown but the truth that animates the
surfaces and evades the senses. And even though you may
not hit every note at its center, when you do we feel where
that center is. (*He touches his body.*) That's why your
playing can't be judged, only remembered. Who wants to
win a prize, be lionized by values I don't value…If you quit,
I quit too.

SOPH
Don't quit.

MATH
I don't want to play without you.
No more practice rooms.

SOPH
But we got into the same colleges and each chose the same
one without breathing a word to the other.

MATH
The very first week of college, you came to me crying. You
told me you'd just had sex for the first time—that things
had gone too quickly.

SOPH

I didn't have anyone else to talk to. He didn't know what
to do so he brought me a pint of ice cream. With one spoon
for us both.

MATH

(*trying to cheer her*) I never cry, but when you do, your
tears try to fall out of my eyes.

SOPH

My next boyfriend said Math and I were stuck in an Edith
Wharton novel and would we do it already, get it over with.

MATH

I won a Rhodes scholarship and the night after graduation
I came to you.

SOPH
To my room.

> *Beethoven's Sonata No. 13 in E flat
> plays. Adagio.*

SOPH

We talked all evening into the night until it was late.
Then—we finally ran out of words.

MATH
We have to—I can't leave and—

> *Silence. They wait.*

SOPH

(*to* SUZE) My whole body was shaking from the heart out. I
took his hand and put it to my neck.

> *She does—just as* MATH *did on their
> first visit to the piano hall.*

SOPH

You could feel my blood thudding. And even though your girlfriend was waiting for you in your dorm

MATH

We laid side by side on your twin bed all night, holding hands as if we were in a double sarcophagus.

SOPH

Morning. The blue had risen but the sun hadn't yet broken the horizon. He was leaving for England.

MATH

I have to finish packing.

SOPH

And as you got up from the bed you kissed me once. Then again. And again. Again. Again. Again. Six times. And then you—we—did the one thing we'd never done together.

MATH

Why was it perfect? Why was it everything?

SOPH

Now it was real. Now it could break.

MATH

You came to the airport that night. You didn't care that my girlfriend was there too. You said

SOPH

My face is burnt by the stubble on yours. Kiss it again before you go.

MATH

My girlfriend fell to the floor and actually grabbed my ankles. You said

SOPH

I can't take it. All or nothing. Don't leave without saying you're mine. (*pause*) If you don't speak now, don't speak to me again.

MATH

Final boarding call. I didn't say: I will return to you, Sophia. I will make my home where I am always in reach of your hand. You are necessary and wonderful. No fear in me can undo us or break your hold on me, on our shared destiny.

Final final boarding call. I said nothing. A flight attendant untangled me and threw me onto the jetway. I walked away from you both. But I smelled you, Sophia, in my every pore.

SOPH

We never spoke.
When he came back to the States, to the city, still, we never spoke.
So I started writing songs for him, leaving him messages where the piano spoke for me.
He came back to me, and now I think he's back to stay.
The corners of my life are folding together.
I'm starting to feel able.
I think—

> SOPH *dials her father's number on her phone.* TURN *picks up.*

TURN
Turner Samson.

SOPH
Sophia Kenner.

TURN
Sophia.

MOVEMENT TWO

VIVACE

> SOPH *is on the phone, continuing the conversation with her father she has just begun.*

TURN

(*awkward, cheery*) Sophia. I've been wanting us to talk. It's good to hear from you.

SOPH

Oh. Yeah, I just—thought, uh...

> *They're silent.*

SOPH

I got your number from Susan. Hunter. She found me.

TURN

Susan? Not from someone else?

SOPH

No. Why?

TURN

No reason. It's just... she and I haven't talked in years. She's well?

SOPH

She seems fine.

TURN

I wonder why she sought you out.

SOPH

You're still South? Last time I wrote you was there.

TURN
No, I moved up to the city fifteen years ago.

SOPH
You're in the city? But this area code isn't—

TURN
Got this line at your grandma's down South; now I forward all the calls to my cell. I'm in the city alright.

SOPH
So am I.

TURN
We've been...

SOPH
And have never run into each other, or... I don't think I would recognize you if we did.

TURN
I'd recognize you.

Pause.

SOPH
I didn't really think about what I was going to say, I just called.

TURN
Then we're both a little nonplussed aren't we?

Pause.

TURN	SOPH
So what's been happening in your—	I don't know how to catch you up on my whole life—

Pause.

TURN
I read about you.

SOPH
Oh that thing in the paper.

TURN
Your singing engagements seem to be getting some attention.

SOPH
Why didn't you come?

TURN
I didn't know if you'd want me there.
We should meet up, and—

SOPH
What do you do? I don't—are you—

TURN
Same thing I was doing when I met your mother. Trying to
change this world for the better.

SOPH
Okay, that's vague.

TURN
(*laughs*) You want hard facts, I don't blame you. I work
as a consultant in human rights advocacy—around pov-
erty, health care, the prison industrial complex. And I do
renovation.

Pause.

TURN
Hey—I just thought of something. Why don't you come
South with me to see your grandmother. I'm driving down

next week. We could drive down together.

SOPH
My grandmother.

> SOPH *shuffles through the letters and finds one. She picks it up, grabs her bag and leaves her apartment for the piano hall.*

> *A beach.* TURN *comes out of the water.* SUZE *watches him. He sits down on a towel.*

SUZE
Is your headache better?

TURN
Still there.

SUZE
Stop thinking so much and it'll go away. It's remarkable to actually be enjoying the ocean with you instead of attempting to desegregate every beach on the entire Eastern Seaboard.

TURN
Is that all we've done this summer?

SUZE
Together. We did see some movies.

TURN
I liked *Behold A Pale Horse*.

SUZE
The acting was good. Gregory Peck and Anthony Quinn.

TURN
About a dream no longer congruous with anything in reality.

SUZE
(*carefully*) I think things with my father are getting better. He's—being decent. He invited me here with him to the convention. He hasn't extended himself at all since—

TURN
(*pointing at someone on the boardwalk*) I think I'm going to keep growing out my hair till it looks like that pink cotton candy. You should do the same. We can start a singing group—The Beehives!

> SUZE *spreads some white zinc lotion on to keep the sun from burning her.*

TURN
Don't forget this part.

> *He kisses her back. It tickles her.*

TURN
You missed this spot too. And this one. And this one. And this one.

> SUZE *puts a gob of lotion in her hand and smacks it on* TURN's *nose.*

SUZE
You're It!

> *They laugh and frolic.* HUNT, *unseen by them, enters the beach and spots them.*
>
> TURN *continues to chase* SUZE.

TURN

Oh, Susan Hunter I am going to get you! You have smeared the king!

SUZE

I'm your fool, that's my job! I'll do it again and again!

> SUZE *does a cartwheel and* TURN
> *catches her feet in the air and picks*
> *her up. He grabs her lotion and*
> *starts rubbing it all over her feet,*
> *which sends her into hysterics.*

TURN

Didn't I tell you not to run from me? It's useless. You've got me under your skin.

> TURN *begins to rub the lotion up*
> *her leg and* SUZE *shrieks. Then she*
> *sees* HUNT. *She tries to jump out of*
> TURN'S *arms.*

TURN

Ah, a weakling who has not accepted her fate.

SUZE

(*hyperventilating*) My father, my father.

TURN

Where?

SUZE

Oh god, oh god.

TURN

Sit down.

SUZE
He sees us. I'm sick, I'm sick.

TURN
Calm down.

SUZE
I left a note that I was going swimming so he wouldn't
worry. Why did I...

> *She pulls away from* TURN.

TURN
You have to calm down. (*a discovery*) You're ashamed of me?

> *Pause.*

SUZE
I'm scared. I don't want to move.

TURN
Go and talk to him.

SUZE
What are you—I don't know what to—

TURN
Just go. Please. Go.

> SUZE *picks herself up slowly and*
> *walks over to* HUNT, *who is sitting*
> *in his swimming trunks, drawing*
> *circles in the sand. She sits next to*
> *him. Silence.*

SUZE
Dad. I'm sorry.

> *Silence.*

SUZE
I'm really sorry.

HUNT
How long have you been sneaking off to see him?

SUZE
He just got here.

HUNT
I'll leave you two alone. I'll get out of the way. You want to bring him back to the hotel with you?

SUZE
No, Dad, that's not—

HUNT
I'll just go.

SUZE
Please meet him. Let me bring him over. Please just meet him.

HUNT
No. No. I don't want to. I came down to swim with you. I didn't know you had someone else here.

SUZE
Please. Couldn't you meet him? He's not what you think.

HUNT
I don't think anything anymore.

> HUNT *exits. After a moment, he*
> *comes back, grabbing* SUZE'S *arm.*

HUNT
If you continue to see him—

236

SUZE
Don't.

HUNT
You have to make a choice.

SUZE
You're making the choice, not me.

> HUNT *stands trembling for a*
> *moment, then leaves.*

SUZE
(*shaken*) P.S. Do you know if Turner's parents are still
living? His mother let us stay with her a few times and
I remember her so vividly. Such a warm-hearted, sweet
woman.

> SUZE *turns away.* SOPH *puts away*
> *the letter. She's at the piano hall.*

TURN
Your grandmother's doing well but she'd do even better if
she could see you. She asks about you.

SOPH
Isn't that a long drive?

TURN
It's a good day's drive.

SOPH
What would we talk about.

TURN
Everything you want to know.

SOPH
Um—let's just—this is a lot.

TURN
Let's talk another time then.

> *A pause—they don't hang up.*

SOPH
This is so strange.

TURN
Hm?

SOPH
You're finally talking to me. Why couldn't you before?

TURN
There are... several factors that—

SOPH
Why couldn't you be my father?

TURN
I'm sorry I wasn't there.

SOPH
But why weren't you.

TURN
Well for one, I didn't have any money.

SOPH
We didn't either. You have money now?

TURN
Enough to talk to you. How is your mother.

SOPH
Why don't *you* two talk.

TURN
It would be nice to hear how she's doing.

SOPH
She's great. Don't worry. She always made everything
alright.

> MATH *walks up to her at the piano.*
> *He's on the phone with his girlfriend*
> *but* SOPH *doesn't hear what he says.*

SOPH
(*to* TURN) Hey, someone just walked in so I'm gonna get off.

MATH
(*to his girlfriend, and holding the key to the piano*) No
I've thought about it and I don't think I should get it. No
I changed my mind, I'm not gonna buy it. I'll talk to you
later. Okay. Buh-bye.

TURN
Take care of yourself, my daughter.

SOPH
Uh—yeah. Alright Turner. Bye.

> *She hangs up, feels the beginning of*
> *release.*

MATH
Wait—Turner? You were just talking with your father?

SOPH
Yeah.

MATH
For the first time since—?

SOPH
Something like that. I was too young to have a conversation with him then so, yes.

MATH
You called him?

SOPH
Yeah, I called Turner.

MATH
You don't call him Dad? How was it?

SOPH
I don't know.

MATH
He's a piece of work.

SOPH
He didn't seem like a piece of—

MATH
No contact since you were a baby? Oh, *that's* a piece of work. But it's all changing. Now you've got a dad. Say it.

SOPH
(*tries to say the word, can't*) It doesn't really—(*tries to say the word again*)

MATH
Say Daaaaaaad. Dad.

SOPH
That's okay.

MATH
He's a firebrand, probably prefers Turner.

SOPH
Yeah?

MATH
Probably.

> SOPH *plays Chopin's Etude No. 1,*
> *Op. 25.*

MATH
You're clicking. Time to cut your nails.

SOPH
Or I can bite mine down to the quick like you do. That's
the only sign you're not an android.

TURN
Susan,

I'm writing this letter in the wee hours of the night. Your
father has no idea of the injury he has visited upon you. He
has injured me. All the energies of my body and intellect
are now marshaled to react to this malignant stimulation,
to act in defense of what I know is right. I love you, Susan
Hunter, and I want you to love me. But I do not want a
love born out of desperation. I do not want a companion-
ship perpetually clouded by the image of a wrathful father.

> *She stops playing.*

SOPH
Relative humidity 16%. Nice and clear.

MATH
You've gotten pretty comfortable here. You must like this

piano.

SOPH

Yeah, but it's also nice to haunt a big room. My thoughts get bigger. In my apartment they sail right back to me before I can finish a single one. How are you.

MATH

Well, I've got some news for you. I see you're sitting down already so I won't tell you to do that.

> SOPH *continues to play the etude for* MATH *under* TURN's *lines.*

TURN

You must love me only because your own will dictates that you choose me. This is the only way for me to be certain of the love that has grown between us.

MATH

(*laughing*) It's good news, don't worry.

SOPH

What?

MATH

It's a decision we've been waiting for a long time.

TURN

Your father is pushing you into choosing me. I do not want to be chosen this way.

SOPH

Stop it with the preliminaries. Tell me!

TURN

If you come to me, come only because you love me for myself and not out of principle.

MATH
If you look carefully you can figure it out for yourself.

SOPH
Where? Here?

MATH
Look around.

> SOPH *begins searching the room.*

MATH
If I'm making you nervous,
I can just leave so you can
collect yourself—

SOPH
Shut up.

SOPH
It's got to be in or on the piano—is it in the bench?

MATH
It's not in the bench.

SOPH
Don't tell me!

MATH
I have to give you big glaring hints at this rate. And medicinal marijuana to help with your glaucoma.

> *It finally dawns on her. The piano.*
> *She looks at the new tag on it.*
> *Instead of SELECTED, it reads*
> *SOLD.*

SOPH
You bought it!

MATH
Taking delivery next week.

SOPH
Oh, Math. Oh. You will be so happy.

MATH
I think I've figured out just where I'm going to put it.

SOPH
In your new *apartment*! Ah! We've got to celebrate! Let me take you to dinner.

MATH
You know we don't do that. I take you. You're poor—

SOPH
And you just bought a $50,000 piano and a jillion dollar apartment! You're poor too.

MATH
I budget.

SOPH
Whoever's paying, we're going out.

MATH
How 'bout next week after the piano is delivered?

SOPH
I might be out of town.

MATH
Where? You didn't say anything about leaving.

SOPH
Maybe—a road trip down South with my father.

MATH
That sounds momentous. Do you even know if he can drive?

SOPH
(*laughs*) No.

MATH
Good luck.

SOPH
We gotta celebrate now. Otherwise it'll be anticlimactic. Let's go!

MATH
Somewhere nearby then.

SOPH
But somewhere special.

MATH
Maybe I can get us in at—what's the name of that place everybody's raving about? I can't remember it. I can't pronounce it. You walk in and they give you a shot of artichoke foam? The napkins are edible? My assistant could make a reservation—

SOPH
Or we could just have a bottle of champagne in an alley.

MATH
No. Restaurant.

SOPH
Where is it?

MATH
I told you I can't pronounce the name, it's like two blocks from here.

SOPH
Two blocks which way?

MATH
I'll recognize it. The sign has a nice font.

SOPH
One day all of the car services are going to go on strike and
you're going to have to actually get a sense of direction. I'll
find it. Come on.

She starts to go.

MATH
Wait—

MATH *plays a few phrases of something.*

SOPH
Is that the Ravel?

MATH
Let's play it.

SOPH
Now?

MATH
Yeah now. Why do you think I bought this?

SOPH *is moved.*

SOPH
I don't remember it.

MATH
Your hands do.

*Under the following, they begin to
pick through a four handed Ravel,
Laideronnette, Imperatrice des
Pagodas, perhaps with mistakes
laced through.*

TURN

Only you, Susan—only you. You must never forget that
you are my life.

With a painful heart,

Turn

SUZE

(*her letter to* SOPH) My father cut me off. He refused to
speak to me. Without money for school, I had to drop out.
I moved to the city to find a job and a place to stay. Turner
would visit me for trysts in hotels on weekends, but everything suddenly meant almost more than we could bear. We
were just 18, 19. Were we already family?

> SUZE *looks at the ring.* MATH *contin-
> ues to play as* SUZE *picks up* SOPH'S
> *hand.*

SOPH

(*to* SUZE) See? He's worth it. He's mine.

SUZE

Then don't hesitate.

> SUZE *puts the ring in* SOPH'S *hand.*
> SOPH *slides it on as* SUZE *walks
> away.*

> *The Ravel climaxes as they arrive at
> the restaurant. "Syracuse" by Pink*

*Martini begins just as the Ravel
ends.* MATH *and* SOPH *are both
drunk and getting drunker.*

MATH

And you know, the saleswoman told me you can upgrade it
for its full purchase value.

SOPH

You can't do that to a piano.

MATH

Well, if I ever want to get something else.

SOPH

Dude, give some weight to this moment. Don't try to shake
it off. Sit in that shit. Sit in it!

MATH

I'm just saying—

SOPH

A piano is a *being*. You wouldn't trade in a person like
that.

MATH

That's what my dad did. Chucked my mom for a new
model. At least a piano will get used by someone else. My
mom, not so much.

SOPH

Let's imagine a world without our parents' divorces just for
one second. Whew that was long.

MATH

Is this a starfish paté?

SOPH

It's a grackle polenta that's shaped like a starfish.

MATH

Do you eat grackle regularly?

SOPH

Ever since I gave up chicken noodles, it's strictly grackle.
Do you think I could trade one of these forty dollar entrees
in at the supermarket for a whole week of groceries? Use
this soufflé as a food stamp?

MATH

Maybe so, as it would deflate on your way. Did you get the
job? That audition?

SOPH

Oh no. I think they were looking for someone who could
belt a little more, sing "And I Am Telling You". My Dick
Gregory was really bad too. Since my unemployment ran
out I'll temp or something.

MATH

You smell so different from college.

SOPH

You too, thank god. Eau de leather jacket and the hair you
never washed.

MATH

You loved that smell.

SOPH

I did.

> MATH *leans over the table to sniff
> her neck.*

MATH

I can't believe something so elemental about you could change. You went from a breezy Moroccan souk to a tropical hothouse misted with laundry room exhaust.

> SOPH *leans over the table to sniff his neck.*

SOPH

Now you don't smell like anything but soap. Just—clean. New.

> *They both move to sniff each other, their noses touch—and they get a static shock.*

MATH

(*laughing*) Ow.

SOPH

(*laughing*) Static shock? Way too many electrons charging up in here.

MATH

I wish I never knew what it was like to fuck you.

SOPH

It *was* kind of amazing. We should fuck. Again.

MATH

When?

SOPH

Now.

MATH

We'd get arrested.

SOPH
You need me to make an honest man out of you?

MATH
That is exactly what you're doing to me. Oh, I was going
to surprise you next week, but now you might be gone,
so—here.

> MATH *gives* SOPH *a key.*

SOPH
Is this the key to your closet?

MATH
Actually, it unlocks the cover of a brand new Steinway B.

SOPH
(*realizing*) You bought the piano to give it to—

MATH
Yup. And maybe you'll let me play it with you sometimes.

> SOPH *is in shock. Then she sees the*
> *wedding band on her finger and*
> *pulls it off.*

SOPH
Marry me.

> MATH *starts laughing. Hysterically.*

SOPH
I know! It's sort of everything—old fashioned, totally stupid, feminist, deranged, embarrassing and totally right.

MATH
I completely cannot keep a straight face right now.

SOPH
Awesome!

MATH
Awesome!

SOPH
Yeah!

MATH
No one's ever asked me to marry them.

SOPH
No one's ever given me a piano.

MATH
You are so awesome!

SOPH
Exactly!

MATH
Did you plan this or did it just sort of happen on impulse?

SOPH
It doesn't matter.

MATH
No, I'm trying to fully appreciate this. You are awesome!

SOPH
Yeah.

> *He is still laughing.* SOPH *is silent.*
> MATH *finally calms himself down a*
> *little.*

MATH
You didn't mean this, right?

SOPH
I'm not sure. Probably not.
Yeah, I think I did mean it.

MATH
Hey.

SOPH
Oh God. I am so...
Take the ring. Just take it.

She tries to shove it at him.

SOPH
Take it!

MATH
No.

SOPH
Just take *something* from me!

The ring falls on the floor.

SOPH
You think I'm broken, huh? You'd fix it all just by choosing me.

MATH
I'm with someone, Soph.

SOPH
Break up with her.

MATH
Like that.

SOPH
You don't even like her. You don't love her as much as you

love me. You haven't even told me her name. What is it?

MATH
It doesn't matter.

SOPH
She doesn't matter?

MATH
Her name's Rebecca.

SOPH
Becky?

MATH
You can't make utopia with just two people.

SOPH
How do you know? You never tried it with me.

MATH
I think I am trying. We're friends. Because friends last.

SOPH
No, Becky will last. Because Becky is mediocre. Becky will take your shit and be proud of it. With me you might actually have to think from time to time.

MATH
Soph, Beck and I—we bought the apartment together. I didn't know how to—

SOPH
It takes months to close on an apartment. You were doing that with her this whole time?

MATH
I'm not easy to be in a relationship with. I can't protect you

if I'm with you.

SOPH
You aren't protecting me now.

MATH
You get the best of me this way.

SOPH
The best of you is what you are throwing away! Why?
Why?

> MATH *struggles to say something.*
> SOPH *jumps up on her chair.*

SOPH
I wrote another song for you. Wanna hear it? Here it go.

> *She begins to sing loudly, slurring,*
> *spilling, then intentionally pouring*
> *wine on herself and* MATH *in the*
> *process.*

SOPH
Why do I love a coward
'Cause a coward's the one I love
Why won't he love my power
'Cause power isn't love and he thinks he's supposed to be
in power all the time even though he's not and never was
never ever

MATH
Say let's get you off of that chair Soph.

SOPH
No no you don't I'm not coming off until you tell me
what's wrong with me. Until you admit you hate me and

then I'll *know* and then I'll change that thing you hate. Is it something I do or something I am? I'll change.

TURN walks up.

TURN
(*gesturing to the restaurant patrons and staff*) I got it. (*to* SOPH) What's wrong, Sophia?

A pause.

SOPH
Oh wow, that voice... it's my dad. Wow Turner hey I'm drunk and getting rejected by my soulmate

TURN
Do you need to be on that chair or

SOPH
So, come here often? I've never run into you before. Never in my life ever

TURN
I was finishing dinner with a funder and then I looked over with the rest of the restaurant and saw you. (*to* MATH) Hello Matthew Brendel.

SOPH
You know his name? (*to* MATH) You're a *famous* coward!!!

MATH
You're Turner Samson? Good to meet you.

SOPH
(*to* MATH) Are you black or white? I thought you were black. But maybe you're white. Or maybe you are black and I'm too white.

MATH
This has got nothing to do with that, Soph.

SOPH
(*to* TURN) You're black. Take me away. I don't know you at all. But your face...(*she touches it*) I can't even believe you look like—I have that whole—look at your hands and your—will you take me where someone wants me? There's gotta be somewhere where someone wants me

TURN
Come on, I'm going to pick you up.

MATH
She's fine, I can take her home.

TURN
Stay there, Matthew.

SOPH
(*to* MATH) Don't touch me! See *he* cares he's going to

MATH
I'm sorry I can't

SOPH
I don't need you or your consolation prize piano. You can put it in your consolation girlfriend's apartment. I've got my own. God bless the child who's got her—

> SOPH *kisses* TURN *on the mouth.*

SOPH
You want me. I've been waiting for you.

TURN
Look what you did to her.

MATH
You did it. You're why I can't be with her. You broke her.

> TURN *tosses* SOPH *over his shoulder and walks out with her as she screams at* MATH *and the restaurant.*

SOPH
Nothing's wrong with me! Nothing's wrong with me!

MATH
You're crazy!

SOPH
And you're *not*!

MOVEMENT THREE

TEMPO PRIMO

> *Gloria Lynne's "Don't Take Your*
> *Love From Me" plays.* SUZE *and*
> TURN *in light.*

SUZE

Should we get married? Or maybe we shouldn't get married. We have so much we both want to do before we—it's been a year and a half. My father...no money. Four hour bus ride between us. No place to meet but hotels. Blurry weekends of lovemaking. All I really have are your letters. Do you love me? Do you?

TURN

(*a letter*) Susan, I don't love you. We're too serious to keep this going. I've got a map for my future; you've got one too. We're slowing each other down.

SUZE

You don't love me? Say it again.

TURN

I don't love you.

SUZE

(*to* SOPH) And the next day he'd change his mind.

TURN

I will love you until my death, Susan, I can't be apart from you. Why do we have to be so far from satisfaction every day?

SUZE

You do love me? Say it again.

TURN

I love you from the thunderous chambers of my heart.

SUZE

And the next day he'd change his mind.

TURN

I can't love you. I am of sound mind and anyone can inter-
rogate me to see my decision is based on practicality and
the uncontrollable winds of romance.

SUZE

Why don't you love me? Tell me why.

TURN

Feeling is a house built in the dunes. It will not stand.

SUZE

I leave my family for you and you leave me? Is there someone else?

TURN

Yes.

SUZE

You haven't been true?

TURN

No.

SUZE

This is impossible.

TURN

There's a girl here on campus. I'm sleeping with her too.

TURN *exits.*

SUZE

That was January of 1966. I tried to kill myself, but I
didn't succeed. Although my psychiatrist almost did the job
for me. Of course my family welcomed me back with open
arms. Of course Turner visited me to say goodbye and our
breakup sex was fantastic! Then he wrote to me of the hard
time he was having finding a *black* woman who could be
both his lover and intellectual peer.

He was not searching for a *woman*, but a *black* woman.
Civil rights was out, black power was in, and for the first
time Turner made me WHITE.

> *She breathes.*

No more calls, no more letters.

> *The farm down South.* SOPH *sits
> outside,* TURN *joins her.*

TURN
Taking the air?

SOPH
Yeah. I'm not sure why I wore heels to a farm.

TURN
Because your mother raised you well.

SOPH
I don't know how you can say that after I cancelled out the
entire March on Washington with my crazy drunk black
lady act at that restaurant. I even lost the ring you gave to
Susan.

TURN
Your great grandmother Mollie's ring? Susan gave it to you?

SOPH

And I lost it that night. I didn't know what it was worth.

TURN

"You don't know how valuable something really is until you give it away." That's what Mollie would say.

SOPH

Around him, I always act like some kinda fool.

TURN

(*laughing as he recognizes his own phrase*) Well, you make an impression. Your family here is impressed.

SOPH

'Cause a city girl can clean bird turd and worms off of some collard greens? It's good to meet Grandma. You grew up here?

TURN

The land was mostly in golden leaf tobacco. Some winter cotton. Tried peanuts, but the crop was temperamental and highly susceptible to fungus. Still. It's our own land.

SOPH

Now the crop is old car parts and A/Cs

TURN

And tractor parts and freezers

SOPH

And trash burning in barrels. Why the trailer house?

TURN

FEMA. River got too high in the last flood.

SOPH

Everyone's being so sweet to me. It's crazy that it took some expat white lady to bring me here.

TURN
No, I think we did this.

SOPH
Why did you and Susan break up? I still can't figure it.

TURN
How much has she told you?

SOPH
Everything she knows. And I don't think she knows that.

TURN
Everything?

SOPH
I guess she's been trying to fill me in since you didn't.

TURN
That's a little patronizing. And intrusive.

SOPH
Sure, but how 'bout an answer?

TURN
Were you ready to get married at nineteen? When her
father disowned her, he forced my hand. Marriage was the
only option. But I couldn't.

SOPH
Because you wanted a black woman.

TURN
She said that? She's wrong. Period, point blank. I was still
in school, trying to understand and define my purpose. Not
even a child could have made me...not then. Your mom and

I married of course. But I wasn't ready with Susan.

SOPH
And you ain't ready till you're ready.

TURN
I never imagined you and I could be friends like this, converse as peers.

SOPH
I'll let you change my diapers when I turn 35.

TURN
You've grown into a stunning woman, Sophia. Why don't you sing something for me. For everyone. Come inside and sing.

SOPH
No.

TURN
You need accompaniment, a piano? Come inside.

SOPH
No. Not...no.

TURN
That Matthew character—

SOPH
(*gently*) No talking about him, okay? (*breathes*) He needs someone to run his life when I can barely run mine. He can't be around failure. And his someone has to have a shit-load more entitlement.

TURN
He wants a white woman instead?

SOPH

Ha. I actually don't know if she's white. But I'm sure she is...Race is a vortex that swallows everything you are. You try to escape, you go deeper into the quicksand.

SOPH *finds a stray basketball.*

TURN

Race is a homonym—it never means one thing.

SOPH

(*almost to herself*) A honomym.

TURN

(*laughing*) Okay. However we say it, race hides the fact that even now I couldn't be with Suze because she gave up politics, and he can't be with you because you're the artist he couldn't risk becoming.

SOPH

I don't know if I believe that.

TURN

Sophia. You know your name means wisdom? You'll figure it all out.

SOPH

What does Matthew mean.

TURN

Gift from God.

SOPH

Jesus, no wonder he's an ass. And Susan?

TURN

Lotus flower. Or lily.

SOPH
And Turner?

TURN
Means Turner.

SOPH
One who turns. I never imagined you. I never even thought
about you. Until I left college. Then I thought about you
all the time. Calling, writing, no response. Needed to make
myself known to you, be answered to so I could become an
adult myself. Why did you leave us?

TURN
I didn't.

SOPH
Yes you did.

TURN
Is that what your mother told you?

SOPH
She never said *anything* about you. But she didn't have to
tell me you weren't around. You're saying she left *you*?

TURN
Yes.

SOPH
Excuse me, let me rephrase—*we* left *you*?

TURN
Yes.

SOPH
And why come?

TURN
Well if your mom didn't tell you, maybe Susan did.

SOPH
So you're not going to tell me?

TURN
Why don't you come inside now and sing for your
grandmother? I know she'd love—

SOPH
You're not going to say? Then why am I here?

> TURN *doesn't answer.*

SOPH
You said you'd tell me everything I wanted to know. Why
else did I come?

> SOPH *walks away but the farm dirt
> and her heels are a bad combina-
> tion. She picks up the basketball and
> throws it hard at* TURN. *He catches it.*

SOPH
Okay. You won't tell me? Then I'll tell you something.
I feel like shit all the time. I've felt like shit all my life
because apparently I wasn't worth sticking around for. And
okay, divorce, separate ways, but at least a call, a visit,
even if you didn't mean it. I feel like shit and somehow,
without knowing you, I grab at Matthew who is just like
you, eloquent and beautiful and *not there* and I feel like
more shit. You may have heard all this before on Oprah
with the curse words bleeped out but I don't care because
no matter how many times you hear it you don't feel this
hurt, this shit hurt that won't go away. There isn't any love,

just pain, loss, absence. This morning as I got out of the shower I wanted to walk out of the motel bathroom naked, show you my body, because you should know what it looks like. Because you should be proud of it and say it is lovely. Because someone's got to. Because if you don't, who will?

> *She begins to take off her shirt and* TURN *moves to stop her. She fights him, and almost has it off.*

TURN
Baby don't. Don't. You're not the one who made the mistake.

> TURN *starts to put the shirt back on her, as* SOPH *cries.*

TURN
When I said goodbye to you, when you were small, you were asleep. But you still gripped my finger hard 'cause you didn't want me to go. You knew more than your mom and I did. Even then. And you're wiser than me now. That's all a parent can wish for.

> TURN *walks to the hoop in the driveway and begins to dribble the basketball.*

TURN
Let's play HORSE.

SOPH
I'm wearing stilettos.

TURN
Play. Show me your dunk instead of your body.

> *He tosses the ball to her.*

SOPH
Will you tell me what I want to know?

TURN
I will if you put it up.

SOPH
You just assume I play ball?

TURN
Well don't you?

SOPH
You're taller.

TURN
In heels, you're practically my height. Put it up.

SOPH
Hardly. I'm not going to *lose*. I didn't drive 11 hours with
you to get creamed. And I don't want help.

TURN
Then you'll just have to beat me.

SOPH
Call a letter when your shot's good.

TURN
I play you call the letter when you miss.

SOPH
How many years have I played by your rules?

TURN
Alright. Ladies' choice.

SOPH
You are going down. Get ready for destruction.

TURN
I don't think so, kimosabe.

SOPH
I'm taking you OUT!

> *She puts it up. Lights out, then a*
> *spot on* SUZE. *We can still hear the*
> *sounds of* SOPH *and* TURN *playing*
> *HORSE offstage.* SUZE *reacts as*
> *though she is being hit each time*
> *one of them shouts a letter.*

SUZE
I saw your father some years after he broke with me when
I was on my way to Europe. It was an impulse. I was moving away for good and called him and suddenly we were
together, together for the three sweet hours before I got on
the plane.

SOPH
H!

SUZE
Once our bodies are together, there is nothing that does not
ignite. It had been eight years since we last saw each other
but nothing had changed. The passion, the passion.

TURN
H!

SUZE
I thought I seduced him into activism, not knowing it was
already his calling in life. He became a radical, went to
prison, even spent time in solitary after being arrested for
an antiwar action.

TURN

O!

SUZE

I went the other way. The assassinations in '68 had sickened me, pulled me out of the dream I'd had for America. I traveled through Europe, met my future husband, and by '74 I was moving to Paris where I'd learned to live quietly.

SOPH

O!

SUZE

But I kept seeing your father for a decade into my marriage— annual trysts stateside that seemed to both confirm and deny your father's claim that our love was unending. I never told Turner I had a husband, but at some point he knew. The bedroom, everything outside it—we wanted them to integrate—but they never did. I

TURN

R!

SUZE

I

SOPH

R!

SUZE

I must tell you that when we saw each other that time before I moved to Europe, he gave me

TURN

S!

SUZE
a glimpse of the life I could never share with him.

SOPH
S!

SUZE
He told me how in those eight years we were apart, he'd
finally met your mother, the perfect black woman he'd been
looking for. He was no longer with her, but I'm sure he
loved her just as I love my husband. And she gave birth to

TURN
I have a child.

SOPH
E!

SUZE
you.

> *Darkness. A couple months later.*
> *Buzzer sound. The buzzer rings*
> *again. And again.* SOPH, *waking*
> *up in her apartment, talks into her*
> *intercom.*

SOPH
What.

MATH
How 'bout breakfast.

SOPH
Math? It's like 9:30am.

MATH
You gonna let me in? It's cold.

SOPH
Why are you—wait a second—

> *She buzzes him in. She finds a cup of*
> *water, splashes some on her face and*
> *drinks the rest. She pulls her hair*
> *back and wipes her face on her long*
> *tank she has slept in.* MATH *enters.*

MATH
Meeting got cancelled and my first thought was: Sophia.
Breakfast. Pancakes and eggs and sausage can change your
whole day. I bet you know the perfect place to eat around
here.

SOPH
Yeah but I don't really want to. Why don't we just stay here.

MATH
Okay.

SOPH
I'll make pancakes. I think I have eggs. No sausage.

> *She starts preparing food.*

MATH
I like the wood in here.

SOPH
You've never been here, that's right.

MATH
I've never seen your piano either. Shall I play?

SOPH
No. (*Pause*) How's yours?

MATH
Big.

SOPH
But you've got the space for it. If it were here I'd have to sleep on top of it.

MATH
So...I take it you and your father caught up after...

SOPH
You can say that. I took that road trip with him.

MATH
How was it?

SOPH
Major.

MATH
I'm sure.

SOPH
We had some interesting conversations.

MATH
What sort of telling details did you pick up?

SOPH
Had a long discussion about magical realism—which he doesn't *like*—he doesn't believe in leaps of imagination like that. Telling. He likes Nelly. (*singing*) "Air Force Ones". But he also has every single record by Eminem. He thinks it's important to *study* him. He drives a light blue Ford Tempo whose stereo will only eject CDs if it's extremely cold and I wondered how long it had been broken and what kind of person leaves things broken. He had serious

road rage. I like him. I think uh, I think we're buddies.

MATH
Huh. You seem so different.

SOPH
I am. I know you talked to him. Before.

MATH
I meant to tell you.

SOPH
No you didn't. But thanks.

She cooks.

MATH
What else has been going on with you lately? What are you thinking about? What's a day like for you right now?

SOPH
I'm temping.

MATH
Should I request you?

SOPH
I don't know if you really want the über-temp. That's what they call me at the firm.

MATH
Which firm?

SOPH
Richards Jensen.

MATH
That's our archenemy. Are you serious?

SOPH

As a heart attack.

MATH

You in a suit too? There goes my romantic *artiste* vision of you.

SOPH

I'm only part-time. I've been gigging pretty regularly, writing a lot of new songs. And I bought a skateboard.

MATH

Wow.

SOPH

I get to be reckless, skate it out. I fall a lot. Hard, on my back, and I stay there and look up at leaves. How they look like stitches holding the world together. Like an atmosphere below the atmosphere, a sign of oxygen and safety. Even though they're thin and wavering, they want to be more than they are, move toward sun, up, out, up...And I'm under these leaves, and the light they let through, but my back is finally on concrete, on something that can't change.

MATH

Go on.

SOPH

I think that's it. I didn't know what would happen when I saw you next but I think I wanna say—enjoy your marriage, your kids. It's all coming soon, I know, so. Be happy.

MATH

None of that has happened yet. It doesn't have to.

SOPH

But it will. If you're not married soon, your firm will suspect you of—not being firm. Rebecca probably works there with you anyway, right? (*pause*) I'm sure I'll love her. We'll all be friends. Friends—last.

> *She cooks.* MATH *looks around her apartment, at a loss. He sits down.*

MATH
You and I can be together now. It could work. You're finally—

SOPH
Fixed?

MATH
Come sit with me.

SOPH
I'm cooking.

MATH
I can't lose you again.

SOPH
I'm here, I'm cooking.

> MATH *is silent and all we hear are the sounds of frying, eggs cracking, pans knocking.*

MATH
(*softly, to himself*) If you don't love me, who am I?

SOPH
(*can't hear him*) What?

MATH
The day I flew away from you in that plane I looked out the window and—

Cooking sounds. MATH, *desperate,*
walks over to her and drops down
to her ankles.

MATH

I looked out of that plane window and I swear the ocean
was standing still. Time just stopped. It stopped the morning we made love and it won't start back up. How do we...
how do we undo that? How do we...can we?

> SOPH *gets down next to him.*

SOPH

Math. Everyone I've been with is a band-aid for you. Then
the band-aid comes off and you are underneath and you
never heal. I finally got some answers from my father.
Found out my mother left him and for a lot of good rea-
sons. But the one he didn't mention was that he never fell
out of love with Susan. My mom found a letter. He never
sent it, but it said it all. I don't want that. For either of us.
No more band-aids, just pretty scars. Okay? I'm letting you
go now. Okay?

> *She stands up to keep something*
> *from burning. Tries some of the*
> *pancake.*

SOPH

This pancake is a little crispy—but fragrant. I thought I'd
try grinding some cardamom into the batter, change it up—

> MATH *stands up and overturns a*
> *glass of juice that splatters every-*
> *where.*

MATH
I'm sorry. It didn't get on your piano did it?

SOPH
No, it's fine. I'll get it.

MATH
I usually know where my body stops, that's strange—

SOPH
It's fine.

MATH
You got it?

SOPH
Mm hm.

MATH
Let me—

> *She hands him the glass. He steps
> back, watching her as she cleans the
> juice off the floor.*

MATH
Oh, I brought this for you.

> *He pulls out her great grand-
> mother's ring and slides it onto her
> ring finger.*
>
> *Then he begins to clean the juice off
> the floor.*

SOPH
You don't have to do that.

MATH
No, it's okay.

He keeps cleaning.

SUZE *speaks.*

SUZE
(*to* SOPH) I am so happy to be with Jean-Daniel, with whom I share so many interests, and such a tender, abiding love. Do come visit us in Paris, or in the cottage in the country! Looking forward to hearing your impressions of all this.

SOPH *sings.*

SOPH
Grow, my love, into the mountains
Grow into the sky
Can you see our love around us?
Or is it in our eyes?
Or is it in our eyes?

MATH
(*to wedding guests*) I want to thank my good friend Sophia for singing for me and Beck at our wedding. Knowing someone as long as we've known each other makes us a kind of ad hoc family. Or something. There's really no name for what you are to me, Soph, but I treasure you, I do.

TURN *calls* SUZE *on the phone.*

SUZE
Hello?

TURN
Hey.

TURN *and* SUZE *stand, phones to ears, not talking. Just listening.*

MATH *plays his piano, plinking just a few notes, as if he's making a melody up.*

SOPH *rides her skateboard and falls. Gets back up. Practices a trick. It knocks her on the ground. She gets back up and falls again. She laughs.*

End of Play.

ACKNOWLEDGMENTS

Gratitude to Sallye and Benjamin Frank Davis, Mom, Ang, Samuel, Larry, Kafi, Cecilie, the whole Davis / Easley / Fisher massive, Adrienne Kennedy, Paula Vogel, Todd London and Emily Morse and New Dramatists, Liesl Tommy, Lynn Nottage, Walter Mosley, Daniel Alexander Jones, Greg Tate, Anna Deavere Smith, Susan Bernfield, Danny Hoch, Kamilah Forbes, Clyde Valentin, the Geva Theatre, Marge Betley, Chay Yew, Contemporary American Theatre Festival, Ed Herendeen, Tea Alagic, Nancy Guri Duncan, Kurt Strovink, Passage Theater, June Ballinger, Jade King Carroll, all the casts who helped me hear and refine the plays, with a special shout out to Michelle and Adrienne Hurd. Thanks to Rochelle Claerbaut and Cameron Stracher for legal counsel, to Bruce Ostler and Seth Glewen for agenting, and to Kate Kremer for her wonderful, generative wayfinding to create this book. Thank you to my students at TRAC and Williams and Princeton and in the many classes I've given across the country; to the Herb Alpert Foundation, Creative Capital, the Helen Merrill, USA Fellowship, Mellon, Van Lier, the duskies, all my teachers, nature, books, music, theaters and directors and audiences for their encouragement and generosity.

SOURCES

Angela's Mixtape

Angela Y. Davis, "Black Nationalism: The Sixties and the Nineties", in *Black Popular Culture*, ed. Gina Dent and Michele Wallace, Dia Art Foundation and Bay Press, Seattle, 1992. Excerpts from pages 317, 319, 322.

Angela Y. Davis, *Angela Y. Davis: An Autobiography*, International Publishers, 1974, updated edition, Haymarket Books, 2022. Excerpts from pages 15-16, 68, 74-77, 83, 84, 286.

1980s commercials for Hallmark, Tupperware, Crave

Theme to *The Smurfs*

"Woke up this morning with my mind...stayed on freedom", "Oh freedom"
Traditional Negro Spirituals

"Asikatali" (Oh we don't care if we go to jail)
South African Freedom Song

"Hare Krishna"
Hindu chant

"Yemoja assessu"
Yoruba chant

"Break My Stride"
by Matthew Wilder and Greg Prestopino, performed by Culture Club

"Ella's Song"
Berniece Johnson Reagon, based on a speech by Ella Baker

"Five Minutes of Funk"
Whodini

"Egypt, Egypt", "My Beat Goes Boom"
Egyptian Lover

"Changed"
Walter Hawkins

"Physical"
by Steve Kipner and Terry Shaddick, performed by Olivia Newton-John

"Don't You Want Me"
by Joe Callis, Philip Oakey, Philip Adrian Wright, performed by Human League

"17 Days", "Computer Blue"
Prince

"How Funky Is Your Chicken"
Playground chant

"Roxanne's Revenge"
UTFO

"He's a Dream"
Ronald Magness and Shandi Sinnamon

Karl Marx, "Theses on Feuerbach"

Aretha Franklin speaks in defense of Angela, quoted in Jet Magazine, 1970

"War"
lyrics from Haile Selassie's 1963 speech at the UN
music by Alton "Skill" Cole and Carlton Barrett, performed by Bob Marley and the Wailers

"I Left My Wallet In El Segundo"
A Tribe Called Quest

"Genius of Love"
Tom Tom Club

"The Way We Were"
by Alan Bergman, Marilyn Bergman, Marvin Hamlisch, performed by Gladys Knight and the Pips

"Fantastic Voyage"
Lakeside

"Black Steel In The Hour Of Chaos"
Public Enemy

The *History of Light*

"Don't Take Your Love From Me"
by Henry Nemo, performed by Gloria Lynne

Dick Gregory, *From the Back of the Bus*. Avon, 1962.

"God Bless The Child"
Billie Holiday

EISA DAVIS

is a writer, composer, and performer. A recipient of a USA Artists Fellowship, Creative Capital Award, an AUDELCO, an Obie for Sustained Excellence in Performance and the Herb Alpert Award in Theater, Eisa was also a Pulitzer Prize finalist for her play *Bulrusher*. Along with her thirteen full-length stageworks, she has written for television, recorded two albums of original music, *Something Else* and *Tinctures*, and directed a short film, *Remembrance*. Notable performance work includes *Kindred, Mare of Easttown, The Wire, Kings, The Essentialisn't*, the musical of *The Secret Life of Bees*, and *Passing Strange*. An alumna of New Dramatists, Eisa has received residencies, awards and fellowships from Sundance Theater Lab, the Hermitage Artist Retreat, the Doris Duke Charitable Foundation, the Helen Merrill Foundation, the Van Lier and Mellon Foundations, and Cave Canem. Eisa lives in Brooklyn, NY.

53rd State Press publishes lucid, challenging, and lively new writing for performance. Our catalog includes new plays as well as scores and notations for interdisciplinary performance, graphic adaptations, and essays on theater and dance.

53rd State Press was founded in 2007 by Karinne Keithley in response to the bounty of new writing in the downtown New York community that was not available except in the occasional reading or short-lived performance. In 2010, Antje Oegel joined her as a co-editor. In 2017, Kate Kremer took on the leadership of the volunteer editorial collective. For more information or to order books, please visit 53rdstatepress.org.

53rd State Press books are represented to the trade by TCG (Theatre Communications Group). TCG books are exclusively distributed to the book trade by Consortium Book Sales and Distribution, an Ingram Brand.

LAND & LABOR ACKNOWLEDGMENTS

53rd State Press recognizes that much of the work we publish was first developed and performed on the unceded lands of the Lenape and Canarsie communities. Our books are stored on and shipped from the unceded lands of the Chickasaw, Cherokee, Shawnee, and Yuchi communities. The work that we do draws on natural resources that members of the Indigenous Diaspora have led the way in protecting and caretaking. We are grateful to these Indigenous communities, and commit to supporting Indigenous-led movements working to undo the harms of colonization.

As a press devoted to preserving the ephemeral experiments of the contemporary avant-garde, we recognize with great reverence the work of radical BIPOC artists whose (often uncompensated) experiments have been subject to erasure, appropriation, marginalization, and theft. We commit to amplifying the revolutionary experiments of earlier generations of BIPOC theatermakers, and to publishing, promoting, celebrating, and compensating the BIPOC playwrights and performers revolutionizing the field today.

Angela's Mixtape + The History of Light is made possible by the New York State Council on the Arts with the support of the Office of the Governor and the New York State Legislature.